Good Housekeeping

complete
YOGA

# Good Housekeeping

# complete
# YOGA

the gentle
and effective
way to health
and well-being

STELLA WELLER

HarperCollins*Illustrated*

First published in 2001 by HarperCollinsIllustrated
an imprint of HarperCollinsPublishers
77–85 Fulham Palace Road
London W6 8JB

The HarperCollins website address is:
www.**fire**and**water**.com

Published in association with The National Magazine Company Limited.
Good Housekeeping is a registered trade mark of
The National Magazine Company Limited and the Hearst Corporation.

The Good Housekeeping website is: www.goodhousekeeping.co.uk

Text copyright © 2001 Stella Weller
Copyright © 2001 HarperCollins*Publishers* Ltd

Photography by Guy Hearn

A CIP catalogue record for this book is available from the British Library

ISBN 0 0071 1039 1 (hardback)
ISBN 0 0071 2379 5 (paperback)

Colour reproduction by Saxon
Printed in Hong Kong

This book is typeset in Grotesque MT

# ACKNOWLEDGEMENTS

To Walter, Karl and David with love and gratitude

The author would like to thank Belinda Budge, Nicky Vimpany, Penny Warren, Jillian Stewart, Jo Ridgeway and Mell Vandevelde.

All photography by Guy Hearn

Jenny Pretor-Pinney is the director of and teaches at Yoga Place E2. Yoga Place E2 offers classes and workshops in different styles ranging from gentler yoga to the dynamic style.

Yoga Place E2, 1st Floor, 449–453 Bethnal Green Road, London E2 9QH
Tel: 020 7739 5195

Ruth White has her own Yoga Centre and runs weekly classes and yoga weekends for all abilities throughout the British Isles.
Call: 020 8644 0309 for more information

# CONTENTS

# INTRODUCTION

The advent of the twenty-first century heralds an era that is perhaps more fast-paced than any other. People of all ages are having to juggle a variety of activities both inside and outside the home; and with the demands inherent in multiple roles come pressures that highly tax and often overwhelm personal resources. The 'tools' for coping with these challenges, however, are within us all. They simply have to be consciously developed and skilfully used so as to develop the necessary stamina for surviving today's increasingly competitive world, and to experience joy in living. And this is why a keen interest in yoga is re-surfacing, and many people are going to yoga classes, practising yoga at home or incorporating it into activities of daily life. This is also why many health-promotion programmes are incorporating it into their routines, and many doctors, trained in orthodox western medicine, are finally overcoming their resistance to yoga techniques, and are recommending it to some of their patients as complements to other therapies.

The word yoga comes from the Sanskrit language and means 'to integrate'. It is an approach to health care that promotes the harmonious working together of all the body's components. Because of its roots in the Hindu culture of India, some people erroneously believe it is a religion. In fact, yoga is non-sectarian and can be practised by anyone.

The most popular form of yoga being practised in the western world is Hatha Yoga, or the yoga of health. Its primary goal is to prevent illness but, if illness does occur, it helps those who practise it regularly to regain and maintain optimum health. It does this by means of a balanced system of physical and mental training. The 'physical' exercises (asanas, or postures) benefit not only muscles and joints but also internal structures such as organs, glands and nerves. They also discipline the mind to improve attention span, concentration and coordination, and they are excellent for preventing an accumulation of tension. In addition, they are superb for improving posture and carriage.

The 'mental' and breathing exercises are perhaps unsurpassed for combating stress, while the relaxation techniques are a useful adjunct to treatments for disorders such as anxiety, depression and high blood pressure.

Because yoga exercises encourage a full focusing on what is being done, they foster a sort of fine 'tuning-in' to yourself. They thus promote a keen awareness which alerts you to early warning signs of departure from good health. They help you to care for yourself in every aspect of your life. Through regular yoga practice, you acquire a keener sense of wholeness.

Many of the exercises can be integrated into daily schedules – no matter how hectic – to prevent a build-up of tension, which often leads to pain. Some of the breathing techniques can be done while driving, or while waiting (in a queue, at the dentist or before an exam or interview, for example), to lessen anxiety, frustration and fatigue. And as you become skilled at incorporating the exercises into your life, you will begin to find yoga more and more enjoyable and indispensable. You will experience a new sense of control over your life as you become less dependent on outside agents to keep you healthy and happy, and more reliant on your own natural resources – body, mind and breath.

This book is divided into eight chapters. Chapter one describes the benefits you can expect to derive from regular yoga practice. Chapter two gives guidelines on how to prepare for your exercise sessions, outlines key principles and provides suggestions for programmes to suit you, regardless of your level of fitness or the time you have at your disposal. Chapter three is devoted to breathing exercises and also throws light on why breathing is so important to physical and mental health. In chapter four, warm-up and cool-down exercises are given for various parts of the body, from top to toe. Chapter five offers instructions for a variety of asanas which can be done sitting, standing, lying or on all-fours. It also includes inverted postures which help to counteract the effects of gravity on the body, and balancing postures to promote concentration and steadiness. Meditation, known as nature's tranquillizer for well documented reasons, is the subject of chapter six, while chapter seven is specially written for pregnant women and those who have recently given birth. Finally, in chapter eight, you will find information about essential nutrients and wholesome food sources from which to obtain them. And you can consult the A–Z of disorders, from acne to varicose veins, and learn which exercises to do and which vitamins and minerals are of particular value in helping you to manage the conditions listed.

*Complete Yoga* is for everyone: whether you are an adolescent struggling with what may seem an overwhelming number of life changes; a young adult wrestling with issues such as body image and career choices; a parent, single or otherwise; a pregnant woman; a middle-aged woman approaching or experiencing menopause, or an older person concerned about loss of youth and recognition, or about disorders usually associated with advancing age, or indeed someone who has a physical disability or has not exercised for some time and wish a gentle yet effective form of exercise that poses none of the risks of high-impact (or even some low-impact) forms of exercise, this book has something for you. It is also a useful resource for those in the health professions and for fitness instructors.

chapter one

# what is yoga?

A system of physical and mental wholeness and personal growth, yoga is based on sound anatomical and physiological principles and so has stood the test of thousands of years. It is an approach to health care that promotes the harmonious working-together of the human being's three components: body, mind and spirit. This chapter gives an overview of the exercises and techniques involved in Hatha Yoga, the most popular type of yoga practised in the world today. It also discusses the benefits you can expect from regular practice.

Hatha Yoga consists of non-strenuous physical exercises which take each joint in the body through its full range of motion, strengthening, stretching gently and balancing each part. The practice of these exercises requires a complete focusing on what is being done, so that it is virtually impossible to hurt yourself. The exercises are performed in synchronization with regular breathing to provide oxygen to the working muscles. They affect not only joints and muscles, but also organs, glands and other body structures. The exercises also teach you to work within your limits in a non-judgemental way.

The breathing exercises, collectively known as pranayama, as well as the concentration, meditation and relaxation techniques, are extremely effective in diverting attention from disturbing environmental stimuli and so help you become more focused. This brings a feeling of greater self-control; a feeling that you are less at the mercy of outside influences. Practising these techniques will also help you to conserve energy and to manage pain and other forms of stress more effectively.

Yoga differs from other types of exercise in that it engages the whole person. Because it requires awareness during practice, mind and body work together to create physiological and psychological (body-mind) harmony, which in turn leads to optimum potential for healing. Yoga is not a quick fix, though, so do not expect dramatic results as soon as you start practising it. Just as the steady drip of water eventually reshapes a stone, the regular practice of yoga postures restructures body tissues in a slow and steady way.

# BENEFITS

## PHYSICAL BENEFITS

These include:

◆ improved efficiency of the lungs and cardiovascular system
◆ less oxygen requirement for muscles
◆ more efficient use of respiratory muscles (see Chapter 3).
◆ less likelihood of breathing difficulties, such as shortness of breath
◆ improved range of motion of joints
◆ improved coordination
◆ maintenance of bone density; prevention of loss of bone density
◆ decreased risk of injury
◆ reduced likelihood of being overweight.

These can include:

◆ increased sense of well-being
◆ increased self-confidence
◆ greater self-esteem
◆ decrease in cravings for tobacco, food and alcohol
◆ greater ability to relax
◆ better quality sleep
◆ improved concentration
◆ reduced chance of depression.

# MAINTAINING HEALTH
# THROUGH YOGA

A growing number of men and women are turning to yoga to help them to acquire and maintain a high level of health, upon which the quality of life undoubtedly depends. They are choosing yoga because it promotes not only physical fitness but mental well-being also.

In particular, yoga is attracting more and more older persons who do not wish to risk injury by practising high-impact (or even 'low-impact') aerobic exercises, but who prefer a kinder, gentler, yet effective form of exercise. Yoga is also ideal for older adults in helping to prevent or to delay the onset of disorders which are considered concomitants of ageing: arthritis, failing vision, depression, high blood pressure, osteoporosis, and so on. Faithful yoga practice decreases the chance of these and other departures from health being inevitable.

Yoga's stretching, strengthening and meditative exercises are effective because they encourage full focusing on the movements and the body parts involved. Used as a door into your body-mind awareness, yoga can teach you many useful lessons for practical application to everyday living: how to conserve rather than squander energy; how to be alert to early symptoms of any departure from good health; how to detect habitual faulty postures and movements that may, in time, compromise optimum functioning; what your physical limitations are and how best to work with them. Through practising yoga you come to know your body on a totally intimate level. This moment-to-moment mindfulness is excellent for promoting calm and control – invaluable attributes for proofing yourself against the stresses of life.

# THE THREE-STEP APPROACH TO HEALTH

## BREATHING AND RELAXATION

The breathing exercises, apart from bringing a richer oxygen supply to all tissues, train you to shift your attention away from disturbing stimuli and to focus instead on breathing processes. This has a calming effect on your entire system and helps you to acquire or recapture a sense of control and self-reliance. You begin to realize that you are no longer totally at the mercy of outside influences and that you do have inner strengths on which you can rely. Practised regularly, in conjunction with the relaxation techniques, yoga breathing exercises help to release you from slavery to states such as anxiety and from cravings for and dependency on health-destroying substances such as nicotine. This is what Edwin discovered.

I met Edwin about 30 years ago. He was then 30 years old and a cigarette smoker. Smoking cigarettes however, was not in his best interests, particularly since he needed to preserve a healthy respiratory system (he was a promising tenor). Edwin's singing teacher gave him certain exercises to do. They were very reminiscent of yoga breathing and relaxation exercises. As Edwin practised them faithfully, I noticed that he smoked less and less, until one day he stopped smoking altogether. I remarked on this.

Edwin then told me that he actually used to enjoy smoking and did not particularly set out to give it up, although he knew how detrimental it was to his voice and health. 'I didn't give it up,' he said, 'it gave me up'. He had noticed, he explained, that as he persevered with the breathing exercises he felt less and less tense and anxious, and did not seem to crave cigarettes the way he used to. In time, he lost all interest in them and, as his lifestyle improved in general, he has never resumed smoking.

Edwin has not touched a cigarette in three decades! Moreover, the stomach ulcer that once plagued him has healed and has never returned – without medical or surgical intervention. He conceded that the breathing and relaxation techniques, along with a more wholesome diet and the fact that he now expresses himself more readily, rather than keeping things bottled up inside, have all combined to make him the healthiest he has ever been.

Regularly practised yoga breathing exercises have other health advantages. That is why, increasingly, they are being incorporated into health-promotion programmes of all kinds.

# PHYSICAL EXERCISES (ASANAS)

Yoga exercises (asanas or postures) are possibly the best tools for correcting learned patterns of wrong muscular efforts, and re-establishing harmonious functioning of the whole system. Because many people in industrialized societies spend a great deal of time sitting – at work, in a car and in front of a television set – the body begins to atrophy (waste away) through disuse. Joints become stiff and muscles become flabby.

For those who have not really used their body for years, yoga exercises are a wonderful, gentle way to bring about beneficial change. They can reverse disuse atrophy because they incorporate full-body musculoskeletal (pertaining to the muscles and skeleton) conditioning and strengthening exercises. Moreover, because the exercises are performed mindfully – that is, with full awareness of what is being done – they are excellent for counteracting the 'scattered' thinking characteristic of anxiety states, and for promoting calm and control. The synchronized breathing required for the proper execution of yoga exercises further enhances this feeling of quiet self-assuredness as built-up tension is released and a sense of being in touch with yourself, at a deep level, becomes apparent.

Perhaps no one I have met can better attest to these facts than Kay. I met her when she was an overweight young mother. During the week, her husband was away at work all day and, living in an isolated area, there was little companionship for her other than that provided by her two young children. Kay, a qualified teacher, soon found herself turning to food for solace, trying to fill a certain emptiness she felt but which would not be satisfied. As she gained weight she lost self-esteem and confidence, and became very depressed.

Then one day a book arrived in the post. It was a yoga book sent to her by her aunt, who had been experiencing unpleasant menopausal symptoms. Her accompanying letter described the marvellous transformation she was undergoing through diligent practice of yoga exercises. And so Kay, at first sceptically, attempted the simple yoga postures and breathing exercises, as well as the Pose of Tranquillity (see page 54) which she did each evening. She credits her teacher's training with the discipline that permitted her to stick with the exercises and not give up simply because noticeable results were neither immediate nor dramatic.

Then Kay's husband was transferred to another town, not as isolated as the one in which they lived. Kay was now able to attend yoga classes once a week at a centre not far from their home, while her husband looked after the children. Less than a year later, Kay was almost unrecognizable: she had turned from an obese, depressed housewife into a trim, energetic, cheerful individual to whom people were attracted. Soon afterwards, she was asked to teach the yoga classes when the regular instructor moved to another town. Kay has never looked back, and she has nothing but praise for yoga which, she told me, brought her back to life.

## Characteristics Common to the Exercises

1 Each yoga exercise (asana or posture) involves a contraction of some muscle groups and the relaxation of their antagonists (those which counteract the action of the contracted muscles). By consciously pitting various groups of muscles against their antagonists, each exercise first brings an awareness of faulty postural habits, then helps correct them, as well as encouraging conservation of energy.

2 When assuming a given position, you visualize (usually with eyes closed) energy flowing into the muscles, bringing health and healing. The full attention given to what you are doing facilitates the process. In time, with faithful practice, this visualization becomes an awareness of internal organs and other structures that lie under the muscles. You may experience this as a pleasant warmth in the appropriate part of the body. Long after the exercise is over, muscular relaxation persists in the form of a 'visceral silence' – a quieting of internal organs, particularly those within the abdomen. By repeating the exercises daily, you learn to bring your body to a standstill, with the spine in good alignment. This is essential for calming nervous activity and for the reduction of wear and tear on the entire system.

3 Each exercise brings into action all the muscles and joints of a given body part. With regular practice, muscles that tend to waste away through lack of use, such as the abdominal muscles, receive a better blood supply and begin to function more efficiently. Muscles and joints that feel somewhat sore and resisting at first, soon become freely moving. They also become less vulnerable to injury and disease.

4 Each exercise involves the vertebral column (spine); subjecting it to gentle tractions (pulling) and/or torsions (rotations) of varying degrees. This promotes an awareness of good postural habits, which is vital to the health of the spine and related structures.

5 Some exercises seem to require a great deal of effort. As yoga training progresses, this effort is gradually eliminated. The regular practitioner is able to achieve and maintain positions of balance with economical expenditure of energy. This ability to retain equilibrium with little effort has important psychological implications: the regular yoga practitioner is able to maintain calm and control in stressful situations, and to act appropriately rather than react inappropriately.

# W H A T   T O   E X P E C T

What can you expect from incorporating yoga exercises – mental and physical – into your daily schedule? What can you expect from 15 to 20 minutes of diligent practice morning and evening, or about half-an-hour once a day?

You can expect your joints to lose their stiffness and become more freely moving. You can expect better muscle tone. You can, in short, expect a more flexible body and fewer aches and pains. You can look forward to having the self-control and self-confidence to deal more effectively with emotions such as frustration and anger, and with states such as anxiety and depression.

With adherence to a health-promoting diet and a greater awareness of the dangers of becoming overweight, the body will become firmer and lighter and your heart will pump blood more efficiently through blood vessels that are more elastic and less clogged with impurities. Other major organs will benefit from the practice of the breathing exercises, which also strengthen the respiratory and nervous systems. Your entire body will be reorganized and revitalized, and it will function more economically.

Practising meditation and the all-body relaxation technique (see Pose of Tranquillity, page 54) daily will help to quieten any restlessness of the mind. It will help the conscious mind relax while maintaining awareness – a state doctors refer to as 'restful alertness'. Among many other benefits, a period of daily meditation will help keep blood pressure within normal limits, and discourage stomach and intestinal ulcers from forming. It will help you to manage stress more effectively.

Step three in the yogic approach to good health, which embraces a health-promoting diet, is described in Chapter 8.

chapter two

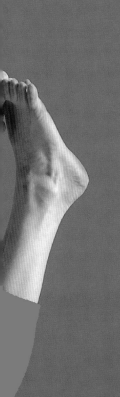

# your yoga programme

Basic guidelines for safe and effective yoga practice are the focus of this chapter. Key principles such as when, where and how to practise are given, and attention is drawn to cautions and contraindications. Special notes for pregnant women are also included.

# PREPARATION

Before engaging in any exercise it is imperative that you warm up your body. Please spend five or ten minutes doing so. Do not exercise within two hours of eating a heavy meal. This caution is particularly important if you have a history of angina.

## WHEN TO PRACTISE

Try to do the exercises at about the same time every day (or at least every other day) on a regular basis.

Practising in the morning helps reduce stiffness after many hours spent in bed and gives you energy for your day. Practice in the evening produces a pleasant fatigue and promotes sound sleep. If you find, however, that practising in the evening is too stimulating and prevents you from falling asleep easily, then try instead to fit your exercises in where they seem most convenient and beneficial.

If you plan a session of breathing exercises (pranayama) separate from the physical exercises (asanas), make it about 15 minutes after doing the simpler asanas, or about an hour before. You may also plan two 15-minute or half-hour sessions a day, or every other day: warm-ups and other exercises in the morning, and breathing and meditative exercises in the evening.

## FITTING YOGA INTO YOUR DAY

Several of the exercises such as neck, shoulder and ankle warm-ups (see Chapter 4), and some of the breathing techniques (see Chapter 3), can be done at convenient times throughout your work day to prevent a build-up of tension. For example, you can tighten your abdominal muscles as you exhale while sitting at a desk or standing in a queue at the bank. You can rotate your ankles while watching television, with your legs elevated. You can slow down your breathing and make it smoother and deeper while driving in difficult traffic conditions, to help you keep calm.

## COMFORT AND HYGIENE

Remove from your person any object that might injure you, such as glasses, hair ornaments or jewellery. Wear loose, comfortable clothing that permits you to move and breathe freely. Practise barefoot whenever possible.

For maximum comfort, empty your bladder, and possibly also your bowel, before starting yoga practice. If you wish, you may take a warm (not hot) bath or shower before exercising, especially if you feel particularly stiff. Attend, as well, to oral and nasal hygiene (please refer to Chapter 8 for suggestions).

## FOOD AND DRINK

Yoga exercises are best practised on an empty or near-empty stomach. The best time for practice is before breakfast. At this time, however, after eight to ten hours in bed without food, your blood sugar will be low and it is preferable to drink a glass of juice and eat something light, such as a slice of wholegrain bread, rather than exercise on a completely empty stomach.

Generally, however, it is advisable to allow two or three hours to elapse after a meal, depending on its size and content, before practising. You may practise an hour after eating a light snack. If you find this difficult or inconvenient, you may drink a cup of tea or other non-alcoholic beverage prior to exercising.

## SETTING THE SCENE

In some forms of exercises, it is not unusual to be 'working out' while thinking of unrelated matters: what you are going to cook for dinner tomorrow, what you are going to wear to the office party, or how you are to meet a deadline. This is not encouraged when practising yoga. Without the appropriate mental setting, yoga exercises will have no lasting value. For the restoration and maintenance of good health, you need to approach yoga practice with an attitude of calm and positive anticipation.

When you arrive at the place where you are going to do your yoga practice, leave behind you any cares or concerns; any grudges, resentments or other negative feelings. Before starting the exercises, spend a minute or two sitting still, with eyes closed, in quiet contemplation. You might, for example, reflect on one or two things for which to be thankful. You might simply turn your attention to your breathing and, if it is rapid and shallow, consciously slow it down by taking several deep breaths in smooth succession. You might do a quick mental check of your body – from head to toe – and wilfully let go of any tightness you may detect in your jaw, hands, shoulders or elsewhere. You might, alternatively, silently recite some inspirational saying, such as 'I will leave disorder behind me. I will cultivate serenity. I will be calm and in control.' The general aim is to quieten your body and divert your mind from its usual concerns, in preparation for the yoga programme ahead.

# KEY PRINCIPLES

### WHERE TO PRACTISE

Choose a quiet, well-ventilated room with soft lighting. Because concentration is crucial to the effectiveness of yoga techniques, arrange to be undisturbed for the expected duration of your practice.

Practise on an even surface, and if the room is not carpeted, place a non-skid mat on the floor on which to do your exercises. When it is warm enough, practise outdoors, on a patio or a lawn on which a mat is spread.

From now on I shall refer to the surface on which you practise as the 'mat'.

### HOW TO PRACTISE

One characteristic of popular exercise programmes of the past (and even of some current ones) was the ever-increasing number of times exercises were repeated, and the decrease in the resting period between them. Relaxation, which is a significant component of muscle activity, was thus neglected. Multiple repetitions of an exercise tend to produce fatigue and stiffness. Instead of tiresome repetitions, therefore, you can come back to a specific exercise later, or try a more advanced variation of it, or experiment with different combinations to exercise all muscle groups. Alternatively, you can give extra attention to areas of your body that need additional strengthening.

Rest periods and breathing appropriately are as important as the postures themselves. Doing the exercises slowly and with complete awareness ensures control of your position and movement at all times, and helps prevent injury. These principles are inherent in the yogic approach to exercise, an approach that represents centuries of wisdom.

## COUNTER POSTURES

As a general rule, a backwards-bending posture should be balanced by a forwards-bending one, and vice versa. For example, after practising The Cobra (page 100) you could do the Pose of a Child (page 94). Pregnant women could do the Knee Press (page 142) following The Bridge (page 145).

## WARMING-UP

Always begin by warming-up (see Chapter 4), and give full attention to what you are doing. This has already been mentioned, but it is worth repeating since it is one of the things that make yoga techniques so effective in the maintenance and restoration of good health.

## VISUALIZATION

Visualize the completed exercise. This is your goal, but not necessarily one that you must reach today. What really matters is the attempt to reach it and the diligence and perseverance that you bring to your practice. Try also to visualize the structures underneath the parts being exercised: for example, the organs, glands or blood and lymph vessels inside your body. Imagine them receiving an improved blood supply and their waste products being thoroughly eliminated.

## BREATHING

Breathe regularly through your nostrils while doing an exercise (unless otherwise instructed). Do not hold your breath. Synchronize your breathing with the movement being performed. This allows delivery of oxygen to the working muscles and helps eliminate substances that cause fatigue. It also counteracts tension.

## REPETITION AND REST

Except when doing warm-ups – in which several repetitions of an exercise in smooth succession are usual practice – do each exercise once or twice only (you can repeat it later), making your movements slow and conscious. During the holding period (indicated in the exercise instructions as 'hold'), do not simultaneously hold your breath; keep it flowing. Always rest briefly after each exercise, and check that you are breathing regularly.

When practising the seated postures, hold your spine naturally erect (but not rigid). Keep you facial muscles relaxed, unclench your teeth to relax your jaw. Breathe freely through your nostrils, except where otherwise indicated.

## AFTER EXERCISING

Finish each exercise session, however short, with a period of relaxation. The Pose of Tranquillity (page 54) is a favourite of yoga practitioners and many classes end with this relaxation technique. Try not to eat for at least half-an-hour after exercising. You may take a bath or shower after about 15 minutes.

## GENERAL CAUTIONS

Before starting this or any other exercise programme, check with your doctor and obtain his or her permission.

Pregnant women who have a history of actual or threatened miscarriage are cautioned not to do the exercises in the first three or four months. If pregnancy is progressing normally, you may try the warm-ups in chapter 4, *omitting* the Lying Twist, the Rock-and-Roll and the Sun Salutations. You may also practise the antenatal postures in chapter 7. But *first check with your doctor.* Not recommended for practice during pregnancy are the lying postures in the prone postion, such as The Cobra, the Half Locust and The Bow. Avoid lying flat on your back after the first trimester (three months) to prevent restriction of the blood and oxygen flow to mother and foetus, through pressure on the inferior vena cava (principal vein draining the lower part of the body). Avoid the Squatting Posture after the 34th week of pregnancy, until your baby's head is fully engaged.

If you suffer from an ear or eye condition, or have an eye disorder such as a detached retina, omit the inverted postures such as the Half and Full Shoulderstand (pages 110 and 112). If you suffer from epilepsy, avoid the Cat Stretch Sequence (pages 114–115).

Avoid inverted postures and rapid abdominal breathing if you have hypertension (high blood pressure). If you have heart disease, avoid inverted postures, the Half Locust (page 101) and The Bow (page 102).

Omit practice of the inverted postures during the monthly menstrual period. At this time, however, the Spread Leg Stretch (page 93), and the Pelvic Stretch (page 98) may be beneficial.

If you have a hernia, avoid The Camel (page 99), The Cobra (page 100), the Half Locust (page 101) and The Bow (page 102). Omit The Plough (page 96) if you suffer from neck pain or have spinal disc problems, and avoid The Fish (page 84) and The Camel (page 99) if you have a thyroid gland problem or neck pain.

If you have varicose veins omit the Sun Salutations (pages 49–51). If you have venous blood clots, avoid sitting for any length of time in the folded-legs positions (The Easy Pose, page 60, for example).

# SUGGESTED DAILY PROGRAMMES

Your daily yoga programme, however short, should include certain important elements: warm-ups; postures to exercise the spine backwards and forwards; to provide sideways stretching and torsion, or twisting, (these can be done sitting or standing); an inverted posture; exercises to stretch the arms and legs and put joints through a wide range of motion. It should also include a balancing posture to promote concentration, and a relaxation, breathing and meditation technique to still and centre body and mind.

The following examples, containing the above components, are offered to guide you in designing your very own routine. Modify them to suit your special needs. The suggested sequence aims to make the transition from one posture to another as smooth as possible. It also encourages the use of counter postures: for instance, a forward-bending exercise is usually followed by a backward-bending one, and vice versa.

## SAMPLE SEQUENCES

### For Beginners

| | |
|---|---|
| Warm-ups | Figure of Eight (page 40), The Butterfly (page 44), Lying Twist (page 45), Rock-and-Roll (page 48). |
| Backward-bending postures | The Pelvic Tilt (page 85), The Bridge (page 86) |
| Forward-bending posture | Knee Press (page 82) |
| Sideways-stretching posture | Half Moon (page 105) |
| Twisting posture | Spinal Twist (page 107) |

| | |
|---|---|
| Inverted posture | Dog Stretch (page 109) |
| Balancing posture | The Tree (page 72) |
| Relaxation | Pose of Tranquillity (page 54) |
| Breathing exercise | Diaphragmatic Breathing (page 25) |
| Meditative exercise | Breath Awareness (page 120) |

## Intermediate Level

| | |
|---|---|
| Warm-ups | Figure of Eight (page 40), The Butterfly (page 44), 2 sets of Sun Salutations (pages 49–51) |
| Backward-bending posture | Half Locust (page 101) |
| Forward-bending posture | Pose of a Child (page 94) |
| Sideways-stretching posture | Half Moon (page 105) |
| Twisting posture | Spinal Twist (page 107) |
| Inverted posture | Half Shoulderstand (page 110) |
| Balancing posture | Balance Posture (page 76) |
| Relaxation | Pose of Tranquillity (page 54) |
| Breathing exercise | Anti-anxiety Breath (page 28) |
| Meditative exercise | Candle Concentration (page 121) |

## Advanced Level

| | |
|---|---|
| Warm-ups | Figure of Eight (page 40), The Butterfly (page 44), 4 to 6 sets of Sun Salutations (pages 49–51) |
| Inverted posture | Full Shoulderstand (page 112) |
| Forward-bending posture | The Plough (page 96) |
| Backward-bending posture | The Fish (page 84) |
| Sideways-stretching posture | Cross Beam (page 108) |
| Twisting posture | Spinal Twist (page 107) |
| Balancing posture | Eagle Posture (page 77) |
| Relaxation | Pose of Tranquillity (page 54) |
| Breathing exercise | Alternate Nostril Breathing (page 27) |
| Meditative exercise | Simple Meditation (page 122) for at least 5 minutes |

## 10-MINUTE MORNING SEQUENCE

This short sequence of exercises is designed to gently wake you up, counteract bodily stiffness after a night's sleep and generate energy and alertness for the day's work.

◆ Figure of Eight neck exercises (page 40), 5 times in each direction
◆ The Butterfly (page 44), 20 to 30 times
◆ The Lying Twist (page 45), 5 or 6 times on each side
◆ Rock-and-Roll (page 48), 20 to 30 repetitions
◆ The Sun Salutations (pages 49–51), 4 to 6 repetitions
◆ The Half Moon (page 105), 3 or 4 times on each side (these can be incorporated into the Sun Salutations sequence: do the Half Moon once on each side, between steps 11 and 12 of each set of Sun Salutations)
◆ The Spinal Twist (page 107), once on each side. Hold the posture for 10 to 20 seconds
◆ Angle Balance (page 68)
◆ Recovery: lie relaxed on your back or in the Legs Up posture (page 87), close your eyes and practise Diaphragmatic Breathing (page 25) for the remaining time – approximately 2 minutes.

## 10-MINUTE EVENING SEQUENCE

This sequence of exercises is specially designed to counteract tension accumulated during the day – at work, in traffic, at home or elsewhere – to promote relaxation and to set the scene for a night of peaceful sleep.

◆ Figure of Eight neck exercises (page 40), 5 times in each direction
◆ Ankle Rotations (page 47), 6 to 10 times in each direction
◆ Single Leg Raise (page 46), 3 to 6 repetitions with each leg
◆ Knee Press, basic exercise or variation 1 (page 82), 3 to 6 repetitions with each leg
◆ The Cat Stretch Sequence (pages 114–115), omitting step 4, if you wish. Do 4 to 6 repetitions with each leg
◆ Half Shoulderstand (page 110). Maintain the posture for 20 to 60 seconds or more. (Alternatively, you may do the Dog Stretch, described on page 109, maintaining the posture for 20 to 30 seconds or more.)
◆ Recovery: practise the Pose of Tranquillity (page 54) for the remaining time (approximately 2 minutes), or lie in the Legs Up posture (page 87), close your eyes and practise Diaphragmatic Breathing (page 25).

Many people who spend hours every day at a desk or computer — often in addition to driving to and from work — experience difficulties in the form of eyestrain; aches and pains in joints such as those of the neck, shoulders and wrists; backache; headaches and 'repetitive strain injury' due to strain on those joints that are used repetitively.

The key to preventing these discomforts, which detract from well-being and productivity, is to take frequent breaks throughout the day and to do simple body stretches and other exercises to reduce the build-up of tension. A good general rule is to take a short break about once every hour. If you cannot do some of the exercises suggested without drawing attention to yourself, look for opportunities and places to do them unobtrusively, if that is possible.

◆ **Eyes** Look at a distant object to give your eyes a rest from glare and a change of focus. Look to your left, to your right, then up and down a few times. Blink several times to keep your eyes moisturized. If you can do so inconspicuously, rest your elbows on a prop, close your eyes and cover them with your palms. Practise Diaphragmatic Breathing (page 25) for half a minute or more.

◆ **Jaw** A tight jaw can contribute to or aggravate a headache. Periodically check that your jaw is relaxed; unclench your teeth (if you can go somewhere private, practise the Lion described on page 39).

◆ **Neck** Do a few sets of the Figure of Eight exercise, in each direction (see page 40).

◆ **Shoulders and Upper Back** Alternately shrug your shoulders, as if to touch your ears with them, then relax them. Do this several times or do Shoulder Rotations (page 42). Also excellent for the shoulders is the Chest Expander (page 78), which you can do standing beside your desk or sitting where you can swing your arms freely behind you. The Cow Head Posture (page 67) is also superb for easing tension in the shoulders and upper back, and for promoting good posture.

◆ **Hands** Faulty arm, wrist and hand positions and repetitive actions can generate wrist and hand problems, and perhaps even contribute to Carpal Tunnel Syndrome (see page 182). Rotating the wrists is one simple, effective way to help prevent such problems (see Hands: Rotation, page 43). The Flower (page 69) is also excellent.

◆ **Lower Back** Pelvic tilting is perhaps unsurpassed for helping to prevent lower backache. You can modify the Pelvic Tilt exercise described on page 85, for sitting and standing positions as follows. Sitting: Sit tall and breathe regularly. Inhale. As you exhale, press the small of your back (waist level) towards or against the back of your chair. Maintain the pressure as long as your exhalation lasts. Inhale and relax your back. Repeat the exercise one or more times. Standing: Stand tall, with your back to a wall or other prop. Breathe regularly. Inhale. As you exhale, press the small of your back (waist level) towards or against the prop. Maintain the pressure as long as your exhalation lasts. Inhale and relax your back. Repeat the exercise one or more times.

◆ **Feet and Legs** Practise rotating your ankles (see Ankles: Rotation, page 47). Follow this with stretching your legs, pushing your heels away from you and pulling your toes towards you. Do this two or more times – it will help prevent a tightening of your hamstring muscles. (Tight hamstrings contribute to backache. See the Dog Stretch, page 109.)

◆ **General** A good general practice is to get up from your chair and walk for a couple of minutes every hour or so. Practise Diaphragmatic Breathing (page 25) during these short breaks. It is also a good idea to do a few simple all-over stretches. Two examples are the standing version of the Stick Posture (page 53) and the Half Moon (page 105).

chapter three

# the mind-body bridge

Although the link between breathing and physical states may be readily apparent, the connection between breathing and mental states, though not immediately obvious, is nevertheless irrefutable. This chapter throws light on the reciprocity between breath and mental and emotional states. It offers exercises in voluntary controlled respiration (pranayama) to help you to cope with various stresses and promote calm. Cautions are given where appropriate.

The ancient practitioners of yoga were probably the first to discover the close relationship between breathing and mental states. This link has now been substantiated and today breathing is commonly used as a therapeutic tool in behavioural medicine to help to reduce stress and bring about a state of calm and a sense of self-control.

Wittingly or unwittingly, we acknowledge the existence of the mind-breath connection in everyday language. We talk about being breathless with excitement or holding our breath in anticipation or awe. We indicate wonderment at a spectacular scene by describing it as breathtaking. And when we're ready to move forwards again, after a period of exhaustion, we call it getting a 'second wind'. When we say that someone 'aspires' to a certain goal, thereby implying hope, we are using a word that has its origin in the Latin verb 'spirare', to breathe.

Changes in feelings, especially if they are intense, are reflected in patterns of breathing, profoundly affecting the smooth, continuous flow of the breath. Fear, for example, produces fast, shallow breathing. Anger results in short, quick inhalations and strong, rapid exhalations. In anxiety states, breathing is also fast and sometimes irregular. Grief produces a characteristic sob and relief brings a sigh. Pain often causes a holding of the breath and can, in fact, produce a change in both breathing and emotion. By contrast, feelings such as joy, love and forgiveness induce slow, smooth, even respirations and a general sense of peace and well-being.

Sudden shock or surprise generates a sort of paradoxical breathing: a reflex action takes place and the person gasps when startled, while expanding the chest and tensing the abdomen. If a situation eliciting such a response arises often enough, the body will in time adapt to this pattern, offering less and less resistance to it. Before long, even minor stresses will produce this type of reaction. And since breath and emotion are interdependent, a paradoxical breathing pattern can recreate and reinforce the original emotional climate – a vicious circle indeed.

Because the relationship between breath and mind is reciprocal, we can create a change in our emotional state by consciously altering our pattern of breathing. I still clearly remember sitting beside a client in the early hours of the morning, patiently instructing her in a breathing technique to help to counteract a panic attack. The technique used was the Anti-Anxiety Breath (see page 28) and it worked wonderfully. Within minutes the young woman had calmed down considerably and was soon able to return to bed. She fell into a sound sleep shortly afterwards, awakening only when she was called for breakfast. I use this same technique myself, with excellent results, whenever I feel anxious. You, too, can use your breath to very good advantage as an effective stress management tool in a wide range of situations.

It may be useful to visualize the mind–breath connection as a kite: the state of mind (feelings and emotions) is the kite and the breath is the string that controls the kite. If you exert a smooth, gentle, steady pull on the string, the kite will in all likelihood soar gracefully like a carefree bird on the wing. If, however, you tug at the string, the kite will pitch and toss, much like a boat on rough seas, as if desperate to maintain control. So it is with the breath: a slow, smooth, gentle breathing rhythm matches or brings about a calm emotional state, whereas fast, shallow, jerky, irregular breathing reflects or produces a troubled psyche.

Health workers in psychiatric hospitals have noted that most of their patients are shallow breathers: their breathing is largely confined to the chest and their inhaled air seldom reaches the deep recesses of the lungs where the exchange of gases takes place. This is to their disadvantage in terms of mental clarity. If you observe someone who is deeply depressed, for example, you will almost certainly see very little evidence of breathing. This respiratory constraint is frequently observed when people restrict their breathing during periods of great stress in order to cut off the flow of painful emotional sensations. Such a breathing pattern tends to become habitual. In suppressing things too painful to remember, in order to render them powerless to hurt us, we also curtail healing, life-giving breath.

The unpleasantness and pain of difficult emotions such as sadness, anger and resentment, and their impact on us, come largely from our holding them back and not letting them through. By directly experiencing such feelings and participating with them through breathwork, you can free yourself from the bonds of much of their negativity.

In childhood we often held our breath when we were in pain. Because we were not discouraged from doing so, the habit may have persisted. As we became adults, we may have continued to restrict our breathing when in physical or emotional pain. What you resist, however, will likely persist. Feelings not dealt with promptly will be stored in the mind as unfinished business in the form of muscle tension and unconscious conflict and torment.

If we learn and regularly practise unrestricted breathing, it can help us to release and eliminate from our mind various unpleasant feelings stored away there. It can do so by facilitating the emergence of denied, repressed or suppressed feelings into the light of awareness, as a prelude to creatively channelling and regulating that emotional energy. When you expose an emotion to light, by bringing it to the surface, you in effect strip it of its mystery and some of its power to cause you pain.

Often it is not feelings themselves that bother people. Rather, it is their resistance to those feelings. If, for instance, you allow yourself to feel sad and consequently express that sadness by crying, you are actively participating with the emotion rather than denying its existence. You can thus feel or make contact with the emotion, acknowledge it and then move past it. If, however, you stifle the sadness, then you risk carrying the feeling around with you, perhaps for many years. This is an unnecessary burden. By identifying the emotion, acknowledging it, feeling it and expressing it, you are much more likely to be able to move beyond it than if you were to resist it and bury it inside. Working with the breath can be one of the quickest ways to overcome resistance to painful and otherwise difficult feelings.

# PRANAYAMA (BREATHING EXERCISES)

## PREPARING FOR THE EXERCISES

Before starting to practise any of the breathing exercises, please note the following points:

1   A full stomach can impede free movement of your diaphragm. Therefore, eat only lightly (if at all) before practising the breathing exercises.

2   Maintain good posture and a stable sitting position. Hold your body naturally erect, but not rigid, with the crown of your head uppermost. This will relax your rib cage and prevent compression of your lungs and other vital structures. It will also facilitate a free flowing of the breath. Sit in a folded-legs posture, such as depicted in the Mountain (page 66), on your heels in the Japanese style, or on a chair with your feet flat on the floor. Most of the exercises can also be practised while standing or lying, and some while walking. Suggestions are given in each exercise.

3   Make a quick preliminary check of your body and relax any part you find tense. Be sure to relax your jaw and tongue.

4   Unless otherwise instructed, breathe in and out through your nose – with your lips together but not compressed – to warm, filter and moisten the inhaled air.

5   Unless otherwise instructed in a specific exercise, breathe in slowly, smoothly and as fully as you can without strain, using your diaphragm as a sort of suction pump and your chest muscles to expand your rib cage. When you exhale, do so slowly, steadily and completely without force, using your diaphragm as a sort of squeezing pump.

6   Keep your breathing rhythm regular, unless otherwise directed. Do not hold your breath.

### NOTE

Before starting, empty your bladder and, if possible, your bowel also; clean your teeth and tongue; and cleanse your nostrils as described in Chapter 8 (Nasal Wash).

### CAUTIONS

Do not practise the Cooling Breath and the Dynamic Cleansing Breath if you have a heart problem, high blood pressure, epilepsy, a hernia or an ear or eye disorder. Do not practise them during menstruation or if you are pregnant.

# DIAPHRAGMATIC BREATHING

If each day you practise no other exercise but this, your time and effort will be worthwhile, for you will be making a major improvement in your physical, mental and emotional functioning. The majority of the work of breathing (about 80 per cent) is accomplished by the diaphragm. Because diaphragmatic breathing promotes the efficient exchange of gases that takes place at the base of the lungs, it is beneficial to all the systems of the body. Consider, for example, the integumentary (skin, hair, nails) system. Skin is your largest organ. When you breathe diaphragmatically, you supply it with more health-giving oxygen and nutrients than if you breathe shallowly. Skin is also an organ of excretion, helping to eliminate toxins from your body.

Other important benefits of the routine practice of diaphragmatic breathing include:

◆ reduction in respiratory rate (and therefore heart rate)
◆ increase in tidal volume (the volume of air inspired and expired in one normal respiratory cycle, that is, inhalation and exhalation)
◆ increase in alveolar ventilation
◆ decrease in residual volume (the volume of air remaining in the lungs at the end of maximal respiration)
◆ increase in the ability to cough effectively
◆ increased exercise tolerance
◆ the up-and-down motion of the diaphragm gives a gentle massage to abdominal organs; this improves the circulation to these organs and helps them to function more efficiently
◆ diaphragmatic breathing is a very important tool for the management of stress; it promotes a natural, even flow of breath, which strengthens the nervous system and relaxes the body. It is, in fact, the most efficient method of breathing, using a minimum of effort in return for the maximum intake of oxygen.

## Preparation

In any comfortable sitting position, lying on your back or even standing, rest your fingers just below your breast bone. Now sniff inwards. You will feel a muscle move inside you, against your fingers. This is your diaphragm. Once you have located it, you can start to practise diaphragmatic breathing.

**1** Lie at full length on your back, with a pillow, cushion or folded blanket under your head. Close your eyes or keep them open. Relax your jaw. Breathe regularly.

**2** Rest one hand lightly on your abdomen, just beneath your breast bone. Rest the fingers of your other hand on your chest, just below the nipple.

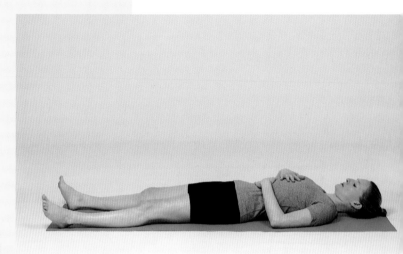

**3** Keeping your abdomen as relaxed as possible, inhale through your nose slowly, smoothly and as fully as you can without strain. As you do so, the hand on the abdomen should rise as the abdomen moves upwards. There should be little or no movement of the fingers resting on the chest.

**4** Exhale through pursed lips slowly, smoothly and as completely as you can, without force. As you do so, the hand on the abdomen should move downwards as the abdomen contracts (tightens).

**5** Repeat steps 3 and 4 several times in smooth succession.

**6** Relax your arms and hands. Rest. Breathe regularly.

### NOTES

◆ If you begin to feel light-headed at any time while practising diaphragmatic breathing, immediately resume your usual breathing. If you are standing, sit down.

◆ If in doubt about whether the abdomen should rise or fall on inhalation, think of a balloon: as you put air into it, it becomes larger; when you let the air out, it becomes flat. The following mnemonic may also be useful: 'Air in, abdomen fat (inflates); air out, abdomen flat (deflates).'

# ALTERNATE NOSTRIL BREATHING

This exercise stimulates the inner lining of the nose by altering the air flow and sending sequential impulses to the two brain hemispheres. It helps to integrate the functioning of both hemispheres, which results in a harmonizing of mind and body, and also greater mental and physical energy. In addition, it is a very soothing and relaxing exercise.

## HOW TO DO IT

1 Sit tall in any comfortable position, with the crown of your head uppermost. Relax your body. Relax your jaw and breathe regularly.

2 Rest your left hand in your lap, on your knee or on the armrest of a chair, according to where you are seated.

3 Arrange the fingers of your right hand as follows: fold the two middle fingers towards your palm, or rest them lightly on the bridge of your nose; use your thumb to close your right nostril once the exercise is in progress, and your ring finger (or ring and little fingers) to close your left nostril.

4 Close your eyes and begin: close your right nostril and inhale slowly, smoothly and as deeply as you can without strain through your left nostril.

5 Close your left nostril and release closure of your right. Exhale.

6 Inhale through your right nostril.

7 Close your right nostril and release closure of your left. Exhale. This completes one 'round' of Alternate Nostril Breathing.

8 Repeat steps 4 to 7 in smooth succession as many times as you wish, until you feel a sense of calm and well-being.

9 Relax your right arm and hand. Resume regular breathing. Open your eyes.

## NOTES

Always switch to the other nostril after the incoming breath; never after the outgoing breath.

If unable to sit upright, you may try this exercise in a semi-reclining or lying position, or even while standing.

the mind-body bridge

# THE ANTI-ANXIETY BREATH

I call this exercise a non-pharmaceutical anxiolytic. (An anxiolytic is an agent used to diminish or counteract anxiety.) As its name suggests, it is excellent for counteracting anxiety and averting panic. It is also very useful for helping to cope with other difficult emotions such as apprehension, frustration and anger.

## HOW TO DO IT

**1** Sit upright with the crown of your head uppermost. Close your eyes or keep them open. Relax your jaw. (You may also practise this exercise in any other position, depending on the circumstances.)

**2** Inhale quietly through your nose, as slowly, smoothly and deeply as you possibly can, without strain.

**3** Exhale through your nose as slowly, smoothly and completely as you can, focusing attention on your abdomen, near your navel.

**4** Before inhaling again, mentally count 'one thousand', 'two thousand'. (This prolongs your exhalation and prevents hyperventilation.)

**5** Repeat steps 2 to 4 again and again, in smooth succession, until your breathing rate has become slower and you feel calm.

**6** Resume regular breathing.

### NOTES

If you wish, you may combine imagery with this exercise. Visualize filling your body with positive qualities such as courage and hope as you inhale. As you exhale, imagine sending away with the outgoing breath negative influences such as fear.

# THE DIVIDED BREATH

**WHAT IT DOES** The Divided Breath is useful when you feel anxious or otherwise stressed, or have difficulty falling asleep or going back to sleep. This exercise also helps to strengthen the diaphragm and the abdominal muscles.

## HOW TO DO IT

**1** Lie on your back. Close your eyes or keep them open. Relax your jaw. Breathe regularly. (You may also practise this exercise while sitting or standing.)

**2** Inhale slowly, smoothly and as fully as you can without strain.

**3** To exhale, divide your breath into two, three or even four roughly equal parts, with a brief pause between each. Make the last part smooth and sustained without incurring force.

### NOTES

If you wish, integrate imagery into this exercise. Try, for example, visualizing going down one stair at a time, to correspond with each part of the exhalation.

**4** Repeat steps 2 and 3 several times in succession. The sequence is as follows:
- slow, smooth inhalation
- one-third (or one-half or one-fourth) of an exhalation
- brief pause
- one-third (or one-half or one-fourth) of an exhalation
- brief pause
- complete the exhalation, sustaining the outgoing breath until there is perceptible but gentle tightening of your abdomen.

**5** Relax your abdomen and inhale. Rest. Breathe regularly.

the mind-body bridge

29

# THE SNIFFING BREATH

WHAT IT DOES A counterpart of the Divided Breath, the Sniffing Breath is excellent for relaxing a tight chest to facilitate deep breathing. Practise it any time you feel under pressure, to help you to relax and remain controlled.

## HOW TO DO IT

1 Sit upright, with the crown of your head uppermost. Relax your jaw. Breathe regularly. (You may also practise this exercise lying or standing.)

2 Take two, three or more quick inward sniffs, as if breaking up an inhalation into small parts.

3 Exhale slowly and steadily through your nose or through pursed lips.

4 Repeat steps 2 and 3 several times, until you feel your chest relaxing, and you can then take one deep inward breath without straining.

5 Resume regular breathing.

### VARIATION

Try combining the Sniffing Breath with the Divided Breath.

complete yoga

# DYNAMIC CLEANSING BREATH

**CAUTION** Do not practise this breathing exercise if you have any of the following disorders: a heart abnormality or high blood pressure, epilepsy, a hernia or an ear or eye problem, or a herniated ('slipped') spinal disc. Also do not practise it during menstruation or pregnancy. Wait for two or three hours after eating to practise the exercise; never practise it immediately after having eaten.

**WHAT IT DOES** Wonderful for thoroughly cleansing the sinuses and other respiratory passages, this breathing exercise (sometimes also called the Bellows Breath) stimulates lung tissues and gently yet effectively massages abdominal organs. It thus helps to improve elimination of waste matter. In addition, it is superb for strengthening the diaphragm and abdominal muscles.

## HOW TO DO IT

1 Sit comfortably and observe good posture. Relax your shoulders, arms and hands. Close your eyes or keep them open. Relax your jaw. Breathe regularly.

2 Inhale slowly, smoothly and as fully as you can without strain.

3 Exhale briskly through your nose as if sneezing, focusing your attention on your abdomen which will tighten and flatten.

4 Inhalation will follow automatically as you relax your abdomen and chest.

5 Repeat steps 3 and 4, again and again in rapid succession. Try to do so about six times to start with. Gradually increase the number of times as your stamina increases and you become more familiar with the technique.

6 Rest. Resume regular breathing.

the mind-body bridge

31

# THE COOLING BREATH

**WHAT IT DOES** When your body becomes overheated, such as during a fever or hot weather, the Cooling Breath is useful in helping to restore normal body temperature and promote comfort.

## HOW TO DO IT

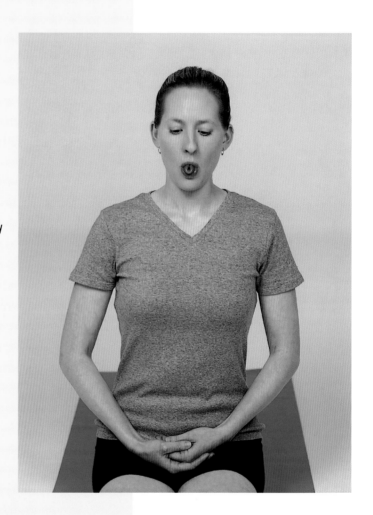

1 Sit upright, with the crown of your head uppermost. Close your eyes or keep them open. Relax your jaw. Breathe regularly. (You may also practise this exercise in a standing or semi-reclining position.)

2 Stick out your tongue and curl it lengthways to form a sort of tube. Inhale slowly, smoothly and fully through this 'tube'.

3 Pull in your tongue and close your mouth, but keep your jaw relaxed. Exhale slowly, smoothly and completely through your nose.

4 Repeat steps 2 and 3 in smooth succession, as many times as you wish.

5 Resume regular breathing.

complete yoga

# HUMMING BREATH

This is rather like meditation on sound. It calms the mind, soothes the spirit and relaxes the body.

## HOW TO DO IT

1 Sit comfortably. Relax your arms and hands. Close your eyes. Relax your jaw and breathe regularly.

2 Inhale slowly, smoothly and as deeply as you can without strain.

3 As you exhale, slowly and steadily, make a humming sound which should last as long as your exhalation does. Pay full attention to this sound; become immersed in it.

4 Repeat steps 2 and 3, again and again in smooth succession, until you feel relaxed.

5 Resume normal breathing.

the mind-body bridge

# WHISPERING BREATH

This is a marvellous exercise to practise if you suffer from asthma. It helps you to gain control of the muscles involved in breathing, especially your diaphragm, which plays an important part in breathing out. The exercise also helps improve concentration and promote relaxation.

## HOW TO DO IT

You will need a lighted candle.

1 Sit comfortably in front of the lighted candle. Relax your arms and hands. Relax your jaw. Breathe regularly.

2 Inhale through your nostrils slowly, smoothly and steadily.

3 Through pouted lips, very slowly, gently and with control, blow at the candle flame to make it flicker but not to put it out.

4 When your exhalation has ended, repeat steps 2 and 3 again and again, in smooth succession, until you begin to feel tired.

5 Rest. Breathe regularly.

### NOTE

When you have mastered this technique, you can dispense with the candle and simply imagine that you are blowing at the flame. You can then practise the exercise sitting, lying, standing or walking up a flight of stairs.

complete yoga

34

# BREATHING AWAY PAIN

Emotions and breath are very closely connected. By slowing down your respirations, you lessen or prevent the build-up of tension. As tension decreases, circulation to a painful area of the body improves and pain-producing irritants are eliminated. Moreover, the diverting of attention to the breathing process itself dulls the perception of pain. You can modify this technique to breathe away other difficult sensations or emotions.

## HOW TO DO IT

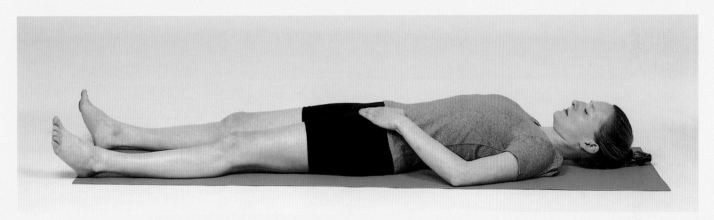

1 Sit or lie comfortably and keep your spine as well aligned as possible. Close your eyes or keep them open. Relax your jaw and breathe regularly.

2 Rest your hands (or hand) lightly on the painful area. As you take a slow, smooth breath inwards, imagine a soothing jet of warm water flowing along your arm to your hand and through your fingers into the affected part. Imagine that the water has healing properties.

3 As you breathe out slowly and smoothly, visualize a washing-away of irritants and impurities from the affected part; visualize them leaving the body on the outgoing breath.

4 Repeat steps 2 and 3 again and again, in smooth succession, until you sense relief from your discomfort or pain.

5 Relax your arms and hands. Breathe regularly.

the mind-body bridge

35

chapter four

warm

# ng up and cooling down

The importance of warming up before, and cooling down after exercising is outlined in this chapter. It includes a number of exercises for various body parts from face to feet. These have the added benefit of acting as local relaxation techniques, and they can be integrated into even the busiest of schedules, to discourage tension build-up, which can lead to aches, pain and other discomforts. For the whole body, the popular Sun Salutations and The Pose of Tranquillity are included.

Why warm up? Warm-ups are a very important part of any exercise programme. They help reduce stiffness, increase body temperature and improve lymph and blood circulation. They also help to prevent muscular pulls and strains once the actual exercises are in progress.

It is also important to cool down after exercising. Cooling down affords the chance for static muscle stretching, which enhances flexibility. It provides an activity for the cardiovascular system to return to normal in a gradual way. In addition, it helps prevent problems related to a sudden drop in blood pressure – such as dizziness and fainting – which can occur if exercise is stopped abruptly.

All the warm-up exercises in this chapter, except the Rock-and-Roll may be done as cool-down exercises. If you wish to do the Stick Posture (page 52) and the Sun Salutations (pages 49–51) as cool-down exercises, do them very slowly. You may finish your exercise session, as many yoga students do, with the Pose of Tranquillity (page 54).

# FACE: THE LION

Wonderful for helping to rid your tongue and jaw of tension. The Lion can contribute to improved voice quality if practised regularly. It is also useful in averting a sore throat or in reducing its severity and duration, and it can help to prevent bad breath.

## HOW TO DO IT

1 Sit on your heels, Japanese style. Breathe regularly.

2 Inhale slowly and smoothly.

3 As you exhale, open your mouth fully; stick out your tongue; open your eyes wide as if staring; tense the muscles of your face and throat. (You may also stiffen your arms and fingers.)

4 When your exhalation is complete, pull in your tongue, close your mouth but do not clench your teeth, and relax your face and throat. Relax your arms and hands. Close your eyes and breathe regularly.

5 Rest briefly, visualizing all the built-up tension draining from your face, throat and tongue.

6 Repeat steps 3 to 5 once more. Repeat the exercise later, if you wish.

warming up and cooling down

39

# NECK: FIGURE OF EIGHT

This exercise reduces stiffness and promotes flexibility of the cervical (neck) part of the spine.

## HOW TO DO IT

**1** Sit comfortably. Close your eyes or keep them open. Keep your shoulders, arms and hands relaxed. Breathe regularly throughout the exercise.

**2** Imagine a large figure-eight lying on its side in front of you. Starting at the middle, trace its outline with your nose or mouth a few times in one direction.

**3** Pause briefly, then trace the outline of the figure-eight a few times in the other direction. Rest.

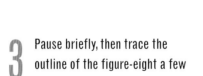

complete yoga

40

# NECK: EAR-TO-SHOULDER

WHAT IT DOES The ear-to-shoulder exercise tones and firms the muscles running from below the ears, across the neck and into the chest. It helps maintain the contour of the neck by exercising the platysma — a broad, flat layer of muscle extending from both sides of the neck to the jaw. This exercise also improves the circulation to the face and reduces the build-up of tension in the neck.

## HOW TO DO IT

1 Sit comfortably. Hold your spine naturally erect. Keep your jaw, shoulders, arms and hands relaxed. Close your eyes or leave them open. Breathe regularly throughout the exercise.

2 Tilt your head sideways, as if to touch your shoulder with your ear. Bring your head upright.

3 Tilt your head towards the opposite shoulder. Bring your head upright.

4 Repeat the entire process a few times in smooth succession. Rest.

# SHOULDERS: ROTATION

Rotating the shoulders enhances the effects of the neck exercises. It prevents tension from building up in the shoulders and upper back and reduces stiffness in the shoulder joints. It also improves circulation in the shoulders, upper back and neck.

## HOW TO DO IT

1 Sit comfortably. (You can also practise this exercise standing.) Hold your spine naturally erect. Keep your jaw, arms and hands relaxed. Close your eyes or keep them open. Breathe regularly throughout the exercise.

2 Pull your shoulders downwards and backwards, squeezing your shoulder blades together.

3 Bring them forwards and upwards, then backwards and downwards to complete one rotation.

4 Do a few more shoulder rotations, slowly, smoothly and with awareness, then repeat the rotations several times in the opposite direction. Rest.

complete yoga

42

# HANDS: ROTATION

The following exercise keeps your wrist and fingers flexible. It improves coordination and circulation, and strengthens the fingers and hands. It may also be of help in relieving arthritic pain.

## HOW TO DO IT

1 Breathing regularly, vigorously rub your hands together, several times, to warm them up.

2 Briskly shake your hands, several times, as if trying to rid them of drops of water. Keep breathing regularly.

3 Rotate your wrists several times in slow, smooth succession, first in one direction then the other (visualize drawing circles with your fingers). Breathe regularly throughout the exercise.

warming up and cooling down

43

# HIPS AND LEGS:
# THE BUTTERFLY

The Butterfly reduces stiffness in the ankle, knee and hip joints. It stretches and tones the adductor muscles running along the inner thighs and also improves circulation in the pelvic area.

## HOW TO DO IT

1 Sit comfortably. Hold your spine naturally erect. Relax your jaw and shoulders. Breathe regularly throughout the exercise.

2 Fold your legs, one at a time, bringing the soles of your feet together. Clasp your hands around your feet and bring your feet comfortably close to your body.

3 Lower and raise your knees, like a butterfly flapping its wings. Do this as many times as you wish, in smooth succession.

4 Carefully unfold your legs and stretch them out, one at a time. Rest.

complete yoga

# HIPS AND LEGS: THE LYING TWIST

**WHAT IT DOES** This warm-up firms and strengthens the oblique and transverse abdominal muscles (part of the 'abdominal corset') and those of the lower back. It helps keep the waistline trim and promotes a healthy pelvis.

## HOW TO DO IT

1 Lie on your back, with your arms stretched out at shoulder level. Breathe regularly.

2 Bend your legs, one at a time, until the soles of your feet are flat on the mat. Now bring your knees towards your chest.

3 Keeping your shoulders and arms in firm contact with the mat, slowly, smoothly and carefully tilt your knees to one side as you exhale. You may keep your head still or turn it to the side opposite your knees.

4 Inhale and bring your knees back to your chest.

5 Exhale and tilt your knees to the opposite side, keeping your head still or turning it opposite to your knees.

6 Repeat the side-to-side tilting of your knees several times in slow, smooth succession.

7 Stretch out and rest.

# HIPS AND LEGS: SINGLE LEG RAISE

In addition to improving circulation in the legs, this exercise tones and firms the long muscles that run up and down the length of the abdomen.

## HOW TO DO IT

**1** Lie on your back with your legs outstretched in front and your arms beside you. Relax your jaw. Breathe regularly.

**2** Press the small of your back against the mat and, as you exhale, raise one leg, kept straight, as high as you comfortably can. If you wish, you may flex your ankle joint, aiming your heel upwards and pointing your toes towards you.

**3** Slowly, and with control, lower your raised leg to the mat as you inhale.

**4** Rest briefly. Breathe regularly.

**5** Repeat steps 2 to 4 two or more times.

**6** Repeat steps 2 to 4, changing the position of the legs.

# ANKLES: ROTATION

Rotating your ankles improves the circulation to your feet and legs and improves the flexibility of your ankle joints.

## HOW TO DO IT

**1** Sit where you can move your feet freely. Maintain good posture. Breathe regularly throughout the exercise.

**2** Rotate your ankles in slow, smooth circles a few times.

**3** Repeat the rotations in the opposite direction.

warming up and cooling down

47

# WHOLE BODY: ROCK-AND-ROLL

This exercise conditions the back and abdominal muscles, and helps to loosen tight hamstrings (the muscles at the back of the legs). These affect the tilt of the pelvis and, therefore, posture. In addition, when you practise the Rock-and-Roll, you press on 64 traditional acupuncture points.

## HOW TO DO IT

complete yoga

**1** Sit on your mat. Bend your legs and rest the soles of your feet flat on the mat, comfortably close to your bottom.

**2** Pass your arms around your knees and hug your thighs. Tilt your head down and tuck in your chin. Make your back as rounded as you can. Breathe regularly throughout the exercise.

**3** Inhaling, kick backwards to help you roll onto your back.

**4** Exhaling, kick forwards and come again into a sitting position. Be careful not to land heavily on your feet as you may jar your spine. Simply touch the mat lightly with your feet or toes.

**5** Repeat steps 3 and 4 several times in smooth succession, synchronizing your breathing with the rock-and-roll movements. Rest.

### NOTE

This exercise should only be used as a warm-up, not a cool-down. You may find this exercise easier if you place your hands under your knees.

48

# SUN SALUTATIONS

**CAUTION** Avoid these exercises if you have varicose veins, venous blood clots, high blood pressure or a hernia. See also cautions for the Dog Stretch (page 109).

**WHAT IT DOES** As well as being good warm-up and cool-down exercises, the Sun Salutations can be used as a short, almost complete exercise session when you are pressed for time. They are excellent for promoting overall flexibility, and help to prevent the build-up of fat. A superb tension-reliever, they are also helpful in reducing stress.

Because the Sun Salutations encourage concentration and conscious breathing, they are a splendid set of exercises for promoting a 'fine-tuning-in' to yourself, so you can be more alert to departures from normal functioning. They also improve vitality.

The Sun Salutations are beneficial to the lymphatic system (part of the immune system which protects you from disease). By contracting various muscles, the exercises exert gentle pressure on underlying blood and lymphatic vessels. The non-strenuous stretching action provided by all the different movements temporarily removes 'kinks' from lymphatic vessels and promotes a smoother flow of lymph. (Lymph eliminates waste matter and provides oxygen and other nourishment to the cells of your body.)

### HOW TO DO THEM

1 Stand tall, with the palms of your hands together in front of your chest. Breathe regularly.

1

warming up and cooling down

2 Inhale, raise your arms and carefully bend backwards to stretch the front of your body. Tighten your buttock muscles to help protect your lower back.

2                                              3

3 Exhaling, bend forwards (at your hip joints rather than your waist) and place your hands on the mat beside your feet. If necessary, bend your knees; as you become more flexible, you will be able to do this step with your knees straight.

4 Inhale and look up. Taking the weight of your body on both hands, step back with your left foot.

5 Briefly suspending your breath (neither inhaling or exhaling), step backwards with your right foot. The weight of your body is now borne by your hands and feet, and your body is relatively level from the back of your head to your heels. (This is another version of the Inclined Plane described in chapter 5, page 103.)

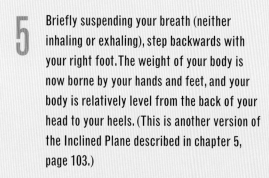

4                                              5

6 Exhale and lower your knees to the mat. Also lower your chin or forehead (whichever is more comfortable) and chest to the mat. Relax your feet.

7 Inhaling, lower your body to the mat and slowly and carefully arch your back. Keep your head up and back, and your hands pressed to the mat. (This position is the same as The Cobra, page 100.)

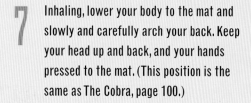

6                                              7

**8** Exhale and point your toes forwards; push against the mat with your hands to help raise your hips. Arms are straight (or almost straight), and your head hangs down. Aim your heels towards the mat but do not strain. (This position is the same as the Dog Stretch, page 109.)

**9** Inhaling, look up, rock forwards onto your toes and step between your hands with your left foot.

8

9

**10** Exhaling, step between your hands with your right foot and bend forwards as in step 3 of these instructions.

**11** Inhaling, come up carefully into a standing position, and move smoothly into the backwards bend described in step 2 of these instructions.

10

11

**12** Exhaling, resume your starting position, as described in step 1. Breathe regularly.

Repeat the sequence (steps 2 to 12) as many times as desired, alternating left foot with right in steps 4 and 9. Rest.

12

# WHOLE BODY:
# THE STICK POSTURE

WHAT IT DOES This is essentially an all-over body stretch done in a supine, or lying on the back, position.

## HOW TO DO IT

**1** Lie on your mat, with your legs stretched out in front and your arms at your sides. Close your eyes and breathe regularly.

**2** Inhale slowly, smoothly and deeply as you bring your arms overhead and, if possible, place your palms together. At the same time, stretch your legs to their fullest extent, pulling your toes towards you and pushing your heels away from you. The entire stretch should be done as one smooth, conscious movement in synchronization with a slow inhalation.

**3** Maintain the all-body stretch for a few seconds but do not hold your breath.

**4** Exhale and release the all-over stretch, bringing your arms back at your sides. Rest.

**5** You may repeat the exercise once. Rest afterwards.

complete yoga

# STANDING VERSION OF THE STICK POSTURE

1 Stand tall, with your weight equally distributed between your feet. Relax your arms at your sides. Breathe regularly.

2 Inhale and raise your arms overhead, stretching them fully. Bring your palms together if you can.

3 Hold the all-body stretch for several seconds, but do not hold your breath.

4 Exhale and lower your arms to resume your starting position. Rest.

5 You may repeat the exercise once. Rest afterwards.

warming up and cooling down

# POSE OF TRANQUILLITY (SAVASANA)

This exercise is a favourite of yoga students. It often marks the end of a yoga exercise session, and it is now frequently practised to promote deep relaxation.

## HOW TO DO IT

**1** Lie on your back with your legs stretched out in front of you. Separate your feet to discourage a build-up of tension in your legs. Move your arms a little away from your sides to prevent an accumulation of tension in your shoulders. Keep your arms straight but relaxed and the palms of your hands upturned. Close your eyes. Unclench your teeth to relax your jaw, but keep your mouth closed without compressing your lips. Breathe regularly.

**2** Focus your attention on your feet. Pull your toes towards you, pushing your heels away. Hold the ankle position briefly. Do not hold your breath. Keep breathing regularly throughout the exercise. Now relax your feet and ankles.

**3** Stiffen your legs, locking your knee joints. Hold briefly. Relax your knees.

**4** Tighten your buttock muscles. Hold the tightness for a few seconds. Release the tightness.

**5** On an exhalation, press the small of your back (waist level) toward or against the mat. Hold the pressure as long as your exhalation lasts, then release the pressure as you inhale. Keep breathing regularly.

**6** Inhale and squeeze your shoulder blades together. Hold the squeeze as long as the inhalation lasts. Release the squeeze as you exhale. Keep breathing regularly.

**7** On an exhalation, tighten your abdominal muscles. Hold the tightness as long as the exhalation lasts. Inhale and relax. Keep breathing regularly.

**8** Take a slow, smooth, deep inhalation, without strain, imagining that you are filling the top, middle and bottom of your lungs. Be aware of your chest expanding and your abdomen rising. Exhale slowly, smoothly and steadily, imagining that you are emptying your lungs by degrees. Be aware of your chest and abdomen relaxing. Resume normal breathing.

**9** Tighten your hands into fists, straighten your arms and raise them off the mat. Hold the stiffness briefly, then let the arms and hands fall to the mat, free of stiffness. Relax them.

**10** Keep your arms relaxed, but shrug your shoulders as if to touch your ears with them. Hold the shrug briefly, then relax.

**11** Gently roll your head from side to side a few times. Reposition your head. Keep breathing regularly.

**12** Exhaling, open your eyes and mouth widely; stick your tongue out; tense all your facial muscles. Inhale, close your mouth and eyes and relax your facial muscles. Breathe regularly.

**13** Lie relaxed for as many minutes as you can spare. Give your body weight up to the surface that supports it. Each time you exhale, let your body sink more deeply into that surface, increasingly relaxed.

**14** Before getting up, rotate your ankles, roll your head gently from side to side and leisurely stretch your limbs. Never get up suddenly. Rather, do so slowly and carefully.

chapter five

# asanas

More than forty yoga postures (asanas), with some variations, are presented in this chapter. The exact manner in which they are done, which differentiates them from other forms of exercise, is emphasized. This precision is what makes them safe and effective in promoting flexibility and strength of body and clarity of mind. The asanas can be done sitting, lying or on hands and knees. Such a wide variety of asanas gives the opportunity to put the body through a complete range of motion.

Characteristic of yoga postures is the fact that they are done in synchronization with regular breathing. The breath supports the muscular effort and supplies oxygen to the working muscles. Yoga postures are therefore done slowly and smoothly. You go into a posture or attempt to do so, at which point you stop. You maintain the posture for just a few seconds to begin with; longer as you become more practised and comfortable. This phase is referred to as 'hold' the posture in the exercise instructions.

During the holding period you continue to breathe while maintaining the posture, and you visualize its benefits: the slow, therapeutic stretch of the muscles; the free flow of blood and lymph; the entering of energy and the elimination of waste products through the breath. It is important to create images with which you feel totally comfortable. In time, with faithful practice, you will develop an awareness of beneficial changes in the structures underneath the muscles, such as organs and glands.

When you feel ready to come out of the posture, you do so slowly, smoothly and with awareness, in synchronization with regular breathing.

When first beginning yoga practice, you may find that parts of your body resist your efforts. Try to be patient and sensitive and your body will yield in time. If you attempt to force yourself, or if you become anxious, you will only generate more tension and aggravate the situation. I encourage you to persevere with the exercises, to do the best you can at the moment, and not to be disheartened. Your efforts will bring well-deserved rewards.

For those of you who have not engaged in regular exercise for some time, yoga postures are a marvellously gentle yet very effective way to reverse the effect of disuse atrophy (wasting due to lack of use), stiffening joints, flabby muscles and poor postural habits.

If you have not been exercising regularly for some time, if you are not very flexible, or if you are attempting yoga for the first time, start with the warm-ups (Chapter 4), then try the simpler postures (listed under 'For Beginners' in the Suggested Daily Programmes in Chapter 2). When you become more supple – and you will, in a surprisingly short time, with faithful practice – you may attempt the postures suggested for the Intermediate Level, and in time progress to the Advanced Level.

It is very important to remember, at all times, that you are a unique individual with your own strengths and weaknesses, and that the latter can be overcome through patience and practice. Whatever your effort, however small, it is commendable and will pay dividends. Remember never to strain. If at first you cannot get into a posture, continue with those with which you are comfortable, and try the difficult posture another time.

# GOOD POSTURE AND SITTING CORRECTLY

Good posture when sitting puts the pelvis in a neutral position, that is, neither tilted backwards nor forwards (remember that posture is controlled mainly from the pelvis). The spine should be supported along its natural curve. The height of the seat should be such as to place the knees level with, or higher than, the hips.

In this example of poor posture in sitting the pelvis is tilted backwards. This flattens the normal curve of the lower spine, stretching ligaments and eventually producing pain.

In this example, the pelvis is tilted forwards, thus distorting good posture in much the same way as prolonged standing does. This, too, can lead to back strain and pain.

# THE EASY POSE (TAILOR SITTING)

**WHAT IT DOES** This posture brings into play the sartorius or tailor muscles which lie across the thighs, from about the front of the hipbones to what we know as the shinbones. These muscles are the ones used in bending the legs and turning them inward.

## HOW TO DO IT

1 Sit comfortably erect with the legs outstretched.

2 Cross the legs at the ankles and, supporting yourself with the hands on the floor beside you, draw the crossed legs close to the body, as near to the pubic area as possible. Relax the legs to permit the knees to fall outward.

3 Sit in this position with your hands resting on your knees, or upturned, one on top of the other, on the lap.

4 Keep the body erect without being rigid, and relax all the parts of your body not directly involved in the movements.

### NOTE

If the knees are not close to the floor at first, do not be disheartened. As the joints become more flexible and the ligaments more elastic, the knees will come near the floor.

### VARIATION

Instead of crossing the ankles and drawing the legs towards the body, bend the right leg and place the foot under the left thigh then bend the left leg and place the foot under the bent right leg.

complete yoga

# THE STAR POSTURE

The Star Posture – so called because the complete pose, when seen from above, resembles a star – stretches, tones and relaxes the muscles of the pelvic floor, as well as aiding digestion. It also helps keep the spine and the hip and knee joints flexible.

## HOW TO DO IT

1 Sit comfortably erect with the legs outstretched in front. If you wish, you may place the hands on the floor beside you for support, to begin with. Take a few comfortable breaths and compose yourself.

2 Bend the right leg at the knee and place the sole of the foot flat on the floor opposite the inside of the left knee. This will establish the correct distance from foot to body. Maintain this distance throughout the exercise.

3 Bend the left leg as you did the right, and place the soles of the feet together.

asanas

4 Clasp the hands firmly around the feet. Inhale. Now exhaling slowly, bend forwards carefully. Continue bending slowly, gradually, and with control, trying to bring your face towards your feet. Do not strain. Note that the elbows flare outwards and are kept outside of the legs. What matters is the effort because, however feeble it may appear to you, it is producing results. Persevere. When you have reached your comfortable limit, hold the position for a second or two (more if absolutely comfortable), breathing as normally as possible during the holding period.

5 Very slowly come up to your initial sitting position as you inhale. Straighten your legs, place your hands on the floor beside you and relax, breathing comfortably. Did you remember to keep your facial muscles relaxed?

6 After performing a forward-bending movement it is usual to offset it with a backwards bend, or at least a backwards inclination of the body. With your hands just behind the hips, on the floor, and fingers pointing away from the body, press downward on the hands, carefully bend your head backwards, pointing the chin upwards and giving the neck a delightful stretch. If you can, slightly lift the buttocks off the floor. Hold the position for a couple of seconds and then release. Relax. Incorporate breathing as follows: inhale as you bend the head backwards, breathe as normally as possible as you hold the position, exhale as you release and hold, and breathe normally as you relax.

complete yoga

# THE HALF LOTUS

The Half Lotus helps tone various nerve centres in the pelvic region.

## HOW TO DO IT

1 Sit tall, with your legs stretched out in front. Breathe regularly.

2 Fold your left leg inwards.

3 Fold you right leg inwards. Carefully lift your right foot onto your upper left thigh. Rest your hands on your knees or upturned in your lap.

4 Stay in this posture for as long as you are comfortable in it, breathing regularly.

5 Change the position of your legs so that your left leg is uppermost this time.

6 Stretch out your legs and rest.

asanas

# SQUATTING POSTURE

**CAUTION**   If you have varicose veins, practise a dynamic version of this posture rather than try to maintain it for any length of time. To do this, alternate between going into the position and, without staying in it, coming up again, as many times as you wish. Be sure, however, to check first with your doctor to make sure that no blood clots have formed in your veins.

**WHAT IT DOES**   The Squatting Posture, practised regularly and incorporated into daily activities, is perhaps unsurpassed for helping keep the spine healthy and preventing various back problems. It is also good for strengthening your ankle joints and keeping your knee and hip joints flexible. It is useful, too, for counteracting constipation.

## HOW TO DO IT

1   Stand with your legs comfortably apart and your arms at your sides. Breathe regularly.

2   Inhale and raise your arms to shoulder level, at the same time rising onto your toes. (If you have difficulty maintaining balance, hold on to a stable prop.)

3   Exhale and slowly lower your arms as well as your body, as if to sit on your heels.

4   Hold the position as long as you wish or can with absolute comfort. Keep breathing regularly.

5   Resume your standing position. Sit or lie down and rest.

complete yoga

# KNEE AND THIGH STRETCH

**WHAT IT DOES** Practised regularly, the Knee and Thigh Stretch promotes good blood circulation in the pelvis and abdomen. It helps keep the prostate gland, kidneys, bladder and other urinary structures healthy.

## HOW TO DO IT

**1** Sit upright with your legs stretched out in front. Breathe regularly.

**2** Fold one leg, and place the heel of your foot as close to your pubic area as you can without straining.

**3** Fold your other leg in the same manner, bringing the soles of your feet together.

**4** Clasp your hands around your feet and ease your knees towards the mat. You will feel your inner thighs stretch.

**5** You may keep your hands around your feet as you maintain the thigh stretch, or, alternatively, rest your hands (or arms) on your knees to help keep them down.

**6** Hold this position for a few seconds to begin with; longer as you become more flexible. Maintain good posture and breathe regularly.

**7** To come out of the position, rock backwards slightly, put your hands on the mat beside your hips and stretch out your legs, one at a time. Rest.

asanas

65

# MOUNTAIN POSTURE

**WHAT IT DOES**    The Mountain Posture tones the pelvic, back and abdominal muscles and discourages fat deposits around the waist and abdomen. It improves muscular support of the viscera (internal organs). The posture also tones the chest and arm muscles and helps to improve breathing – through which body cells receive oxygen. In addition, it promotes good circulation.

## HOW TO DO IT

1 Sit tall in any comfortable folded-legs position, such as the Easy Pose (page 60). Breathe regularly.

2 Inhale and stretch your arms overhead, keeping them close to your ears. Press your palms together if you can.

3 Hold this position for as long as you comfortably can, breathing regularly.

4 Exhale and lower your arms; resume your starting position. Rest.

### NOTE

You may practise the Mountain Posture in any comfortable sitting position, or while sitting on a bench or stool.

complete yoga

66

# COW HEAD POSTURE

**WHAT IT DOES** This posture is excellent for helping prevent stiffness of the shoulder, arm and leg joints, and thus keeps them flexible. It is also splendid for counteracting the effects of poor postural habits. Cultivating good posture is one positive step to take towards attaining and maintaining good overall health.

## HOW TO DO IT

1 Sit on your heels, Japanese style. Breathe regularly.

2 Reach over your right shoulder with your right hand. Keep your elbow pointing upwards rather than forwards, and your arm close to your ear.

3 With your left hand, reach behind your back from below, and interlock your fingers with those of your right hand. Maintain a naturally erect posture and breathe regularly throughout the exercise. Hold this position as long as you comfortably can. Do not hold your breath.

4 Resume your starting position. Shrug your shoulders a few times or rotate them if you wish. Rest briefly.

5 Repeat steps 2 to 4, changing the position of your arms and hands (substitute the word 'left' for 'right' and vice versa in the instructions).

### NOTE

You can practise the Cow Head Posture while standing, sitting on a stool or bench, or in a folded-legs position. If you are unable to interlock your fingers as described in step 3, use a scarf, belt or other suitable item as an extension to your arms. Toss one end over your shoulder and reach behind and below to grasp the other end. Pull upwards with your upper hand and downwards with your lower.

asanas

67

# ANGLE BALANCE

The Angle Balance is excellent for toning and strengthening the abdominal muscles, and thus for providing effective support for abdominal structures such as the stomach and intestines. Strong abdominal muscles are also imperative for a healthy back. The Angle Balance is, moreover, a superb exercise for helping to prevent constipation. Because it is a balancing exercise, it develops concentration and has a calming effect on the system.

## HOW TO DO IT

**1** Sit with your legs bent and the soles of your feet flat on the mat. Breathe regularly.

**2** Tilt backwards so that you balance on your bottom; bring your legs closer to your body and lift your feet off the mat (use your hands to help, if necessary). Keep breathing regularly and give full attention to what you are doing; it will help you to maintain balance.

**3** Stretch out your arms so that they are parallel to the mat.

**4** Begin to straighten your legs but do not strain. (As you straighten your legs you will need to adjust your degree of tilt to maintain balance.)

**5** Hold the completed position for a few seconds to begin with, breathing regularly. As you become more practised, hold the position longer.

**6** Slowly and carefully return to your starting position.

**7** Sit or lie down and rest.

# THE FLOWER

**WHAT IT DOES** The Flower is an excellent exercise for improving blood circulation to your hands and fingernails. It helps keep your fingers supple and young looking. It also helps prevent tension from building up in your hands.

## HOW TO DO IT

1 Sit naturally upright on your mat. (You may also practise the exercise sitting on a chair, standing or lying.) Breathe regularly.

2 Hold your hands, made into tight fists, in front of you (do not simultaneously clench your teeth; keep your jaw relaxed and breathe regularly).

3 Slowly, and with resistance, open your hands. Think of them as tightly-closed, sleeping buds opening up unwillingly to the rays of the morning sun.

4 When your hands are fully open, give your fingers a final stretch until they arch backward. Stretch your arms sideways as far as they will go, and hold the open-arms position for a few seconds.

5 Relax your arms and hands.

asanas

# STANDING AND WALKING

## STANDING

When we talk of poor posture, we generally mean slack posture. To correct this, there may be a tendency to cultivate posture that is excessively rigid, and this could result in tense muscles and restricted breathing.

In correct standing (right), the chin is in, the head up (crown uppermost), the back flattened and the pelvis straight (neutral position). The rib cage is full and round to permit adequate ventilation of the lungs and to prevent pressure on internal organs.

In a strained position (below right), the pelvis tilts forward, thus increasing the spinal curves and strain on joints and ligaments. The chin is out and the ribs are down, causing pressure on internal organs. The lower back is arched (swayback). This is the most common type of poor posture in a standing position.

Even when standing correctly, there is tremendous pressure on lumbar discs – about 182 pounds per square inch on the third lumbar disc. Avoid standing, therefore, if you can sit, walk or squat. When you must stand, rest one foot on a convenient prop such as a box.

## WALKING

Stand tall to reduce stress. Relax your shoulders. Flatten your shoulder blades. Tighten your abdominal and buttock muscles to help to tuck your bottom in. Distribute your body weight equally between your feet. Breathe regularly. Swing your arms effortlessly. Move your legs from your hip joints.

When walking up stairs, plant the whole foot on the stair instead of the tiptoes. It will exercise your ankle and conserve energy.

# PRAYER POSTURE

**WHAT IT DOES**   When you are in this position your chest is full and round, facilitating deep breathing. The abdomen is given its greatest length and pelvic organs are relieved of pressure from above. The Prayer Posture encourages good spinal alignment; helps to correct postural defects; encourages muscular coordination and balance; facilitates even distribution of the body's weight along the spinal column, and so helps to prevent fatigue. It also promotes physical and mental steadiness.

## HOW TO DO IT

1 Stand as tall as you can, without rising onto your toes, with your feet close together and parallel to each other.

2 Check that your chin is neither tucked down nor jutting forwards and that your shoulder blades are flat.

3 Tilt your pelvis to prevent any exaggeration of the spinal curve at the small of your back (the lumbar arch).

4 Keep your knees straight but not stiff; keep your legs together.

5 Bring your hands together in front of your breastbone (in prayer position). Relax your facial muscles and jaw; breathe regularly. Focus your attention on an object in front of you or on your breathing, to help keep you steady.

6 Maintain this position for a minute or two to begin with; longer as you become more comfortable with it.

# THE TREE

**WHAT IT DOES** This is an excellent posture for cultivating nerve-muscle coordination, balance, alertness and nerve control.

## HOW TO DO IT

1 Stand tall, with your feet close together and parallel to each other. Establish good posture (see page 70) and breathe regularly. Keep your eyes open.

2 Lift one leg and, with the help of your hands, place the sole of your foot against the inner aspect of your opposite thigh. Bring your hands together in front of your breastbone.

3 Maintain this position for as long as you comfortably can, breathing regularly and focusing your attention on the breathing process.

4 When you are ready to come out of the position, straighten your bent leg and resume your starting position. Relax your hands at your sides.

5 Repeat the exercise, balancing this time on your other foot.

complete yoga

# HOLY FIG TREE POSTURE

Simple though it seems, this posture is surprisingly energizing. It helps to clear respiratory passages and improve circulation. Because it involves balancing, the Holy Fig Tree Posture is excellent for improving concentration and coordination.

## HOW TO DO IT

1 Stand tall. Breathe regularly.

2 Shift your weight onto your left foot. Raise your left arm straight upwards, keeping it alongside your ear.

3 Lift your right foot; point it backwards, keeping the leg as straight as you can. Remain standing tall.

4 Stretch your right arm to the side, at about shoulder level.

5 Hold the posture for as long as you are comfortable in it, breathing regularly.

6 Return to your starting position. Rest.

7 Repeat the exercise (steps 2 to 6), substituting the word 'left' for 'right' and vice versa in the instructions.

NOTE

Focus your attention on a still object, such as a vase of flowers or a picture on a wall, to help you to maintain your balance.

73

# TOE-FINGER POSTURE

**WHAT IT DOES** This posture cultivates nerve-muscle coordination, balance, alertness and nerve control. It also tones and strengthens the leg muscles.

## HOW TO DO IT

1 Stand tall and breathe regularly.

2 Shift your weight onto one foot. Exhale and carefully lift the other foot; bring it towards you.

3 Grasp the toes of the raised foot with one or both hands. (If you use one hand, swing the other hand to the side to help you to maintain your balance.)

4 Holding your toes securely, straighten your raised leg, alert for any hint of strain on your hamstring muscles.

5 Stay in the posture for as long as you comfortably can, breathing regularly.

6 Bend your raised leg, release your hold on the toes and return to your starting position.

complete yoga

**7** Rest briefly.

**8** Repeat the exercise (steps 2 to 6), standing
on the other foot this time. Rest afterwards.

### VARIATIONS

1 Stand tall and breathe regularly.
2 Shift your weight onto one foot.
3 Raise the other foot and grasp the toes with one hand only. Swing the other hand
   sideways to help you maintain your balance.
4 Carefully straighten the raised leg.
5 Slowly and with control bring the raised leg to the side, as far as you comfortably can.
6 Hold the posture for as long as you can or are comfortable in it, breathing regularly.
7 Slowly bring the raised leg back to the front.
8 Carefully resume your starting position. Rest briefly.
9 Repeat the exercise with the other leg (steps 2 to 8).

This pose can also be practised sitting or lying. When practising the standing and sitting
versions of this posture, fix your gaze on a still object, such as a door handle, a picture on a
wall or an ornament, to help you to keep focused and so maintain your balance. Concentrating
on your slow, smooth breathing is also useful.

asanas

75

# BALANCE POSTURE

**WHAT IT DOES** This posture develops and enhances concentration, nerve-muscle coordination and alertness. It also conditions the quadriceps muscles of the thighs, which help to straighten the knees.

## HOW TO DO IT

1 Stand tall, with your feet comfortably but not too far apart, and your body weight equally distributed. Breathe regularly.

2 Shift your weight onto your left foot. Focus attention on your breathing to help you to keep your balance.

3 Bend your right leg and point your foot backwards; grasp your foot with your right hand and bring it as close to your buttocks as you can with absolute comfort.

4 Keep breathing regularly and raise your left arm upwards to help you to maintain balance.

5 Hold the position as long as you wish or can, remembering to breathe regularly and to focus attention on the flow of your breath to help keep you steady.

6 Slowly resume your starting position. Rest briefly.

7 Repeat steps 2 to 6, balancing on the right foot this time. Relax at the end of the exercise.

# EAGLE POSTURE

**WHAT IT DOES** The Eagle Posture provides an opportunity to exercise all the joints of your arms and legs. This promotes suppleness and elasticity of these joints, thus counteracting any tendency to stiffness and limited functioning. Since it involves balancing, the Eagle Posture also helps to develop and enhance concentration, nerve-muscle coordination and alertness.

## HOW TO DO IT

1 Stand naturally erect. Relax your arms at your sides. Keep your eyes open and breathe regularly throughout the exercise.

2 Slowly lift your right leg. Do so with awareness so that you maintain your balance.

3 Cross your right leg over your left and hook your toes around your left lower leg. Adjust your posture to facilitate these movements.

4 When your stance is secure, try to straighten your body without putting unnecessary pressure on your left leg.

5 Now bend your right arm and position it in front of you.

6 Do the same with your left arm, placing it within your bent right arm and rotating your wrists until your palms are together.

7 Hold this position as long as you comfortably can. If you focus attention on your regular breathing it will help you maintain balance.

8 When you are ready to come out of the position, do so slowly and with awareness. Rest.

9 Repeat steps 2 to 8, changing leg and arms (substitute the word 'left' for 'right' and vice versa).

# CHEST EXPANDER

**WHAT IT DOES** The Chest Expander is superb for reducing the build-up of tension in your shoulders and upper back. Practise it periodically throughout your work day if you spend a lot of time sitting at a desk or engaged in activities that require you to bend forwards. It also helps to improve posture and facilitates deep breathing (through which every cell of your body receives oxygen).

## HOW TO DO IT

1 Stand tall with your feet comfortably apart and your arms at your sides. Breathe regularly.

2 Inhale and raise your arms sideways to shoulder level; turn your palms downwards.

3 Exhale and lower your arms. Swing them behind you and interlace the fingers of both hands. Keep breathing regularly.

4 With fingers still interlaced, raise your arms upwards to their comfortable limit; keep them straight.

5 Hold this position for as long as you comfortably can. Do not hold your breath.

6 Slowly lower your arms, unlock your fingers and relax. You may shrug or rotate your shoulders a few times. Rest.

complete yoga

# ABDOMINAL LIFT

**CAUTION** Do not practise this exercise if you have high blood pressure, an ulcer of the stomach or intestine (peptic ulcer), a heart problem or a hernia. Omit it also during menstruation and pregnancy. In any case, check with your doctor before attempting this posture. Always practise this exercise on an empty or near-empty stomach; never immediately after eating.

**WHAT IT DOES** The Abdominal Lift is excellent for toning and firming your abdominal muscles, which support your abdominal organs and other internal structures. Healthy abdominal muscles also play a part in maintaining the health of your back.

## HOW TO DO IT

1 Stand with your feet about 25 centimetres (10 inches) apart. Bend your knees and turn them slightly outwards, as if preparing to sit.

2 Place your hands on their respective thighs. Keep your torso as erect as you comfortably can and breathe regularly.

3 Exhale and with the air still expelled, briskly pull in your abdomen, as if to touch your spine with it, and also pull it upwards, towards your ribs.

4 Hold the abdominal contraction until you feel the urge to inhale.

5 Inhale and straighten yourself. Rest briefly, resuming normal breathing.

6 Repeat the exercise once, if you wish. You can also repeat it later.

# GOOD DAILY POSTURE: LYING DOWN

When you lie down, you relieve your spine of much of your body weight. This reduces compression on the discs. Experiment with lying positions to find those that are most restful for you. Lie either on your back (supine) or on your side. Avoid lying on your abdomen (prone), as it places unnecessary strain on your lower spine. When you do have to lie prone, however, place a small pillow or cushion under your hips. It will prevent exaggeration of the spinal arch and reduce tension of the back muscles.

In the supine position, you can bend your knees and rest the soles of your feet flat on the surface on which you are lying. You may experiment with inserting a large cushion, pillow or bolster under the bent knees. This is a very relaxing position for the back – one recommended by many orthopaedic specialists.

I sometimes lie with my knees together and bent, soles flat on the mat or sofa or bed, and feet about hip-width apart. I find this easier to maintain for a longer time than if the knees were apart.

To counteract neck strain resulting from too much looking downwards, try rolling a towel, like a sausage, and putting it under your neck as you lie on your back for half-an-hour or so. You may also arrange the rolled towel like a collar to prevent your head from rolling to the side.

Consider using a feather or kapok pillow, which moulds itself to the contour of the head and neck while giving support and promoting relaxation. A foam pillow, by contrast, has recoil which tends to produce a certain amount of neck tension. Your mattress should be firm yet able to conform to your body's contour without sagging.

When lying on your side, place a small pillow or cushion between your knees to prevent your hips from rotating and your spine from twisting. Both legs, or only the top one, may be bent for maximum comfort.

# GOOD DAILY POSTURE: GETTING UP

Never get up in a rush. Avoid getting straight up from a supine position. Instead, roll onto your side, bend your knees, bring them closer to your chest and use your hands to help push you onto your hip (below).

Slowly pivot yourself until you are sitting evenly on your bottom, then slowly stand up. Breathe regularly all the while, to help you to concentrate on what you are doing.

# THE KNEE PRESS

**WHAT IT DOES** This posture strengthens the abdominal muscles and the muscles of the neck, shoulders and back. It relieves back strain and backache, and also helps dispel gas from the stomach and intestines.

## HOW TO DO IT

1 Lie on your back, legs outstretched in front and arms alongside the body. Keep the small of the back pressed to the floor as much as possible.

2 Exhaling, bend one leg and bring the bent knee towards you. Clasp your hands around the bent knee. This is the basic knee press.

3 Hold the position for a few seconds, breathing normally.

4 Inhaling, slowly release the hold on the leg and gradually lower it to the floor. Keep the small of the back pressed to the floor.

5 Relax for a few seconds, breathing normally.

6 Repeat steps 2 to 5, bending the other leg this time.

## VARIATION 1

1   Follow steps 1 and 2.
2   Bend your head forwards and try to touch the bent knee with it.
3   Hold the position for a few seconds, breathing as normally as you can.
4   Release the hold on the leg and carefully lower arms, head, then leg to the floor. Relax, breathing normally.
5   Repeat with the other leg.

## VARIATION 2

1   Lie as described in step 1.
2   Exhaling, bend one leg and bring the knee towards you. Continue breathing regularly.
3   Again on an exhalation, bend your other leg and bring it towards you. Continue breathing regularly. Hold the bent legs securely.
4   Carefully raise your head and bring your forehead towards the bent knees as you exhale. Keep your shoulders as relaxed as possible.
5   Hold the position as long as you comfortably can, breathing regularly.
6   Carefully lower your head to the mat.
7   Release the hold on each leg in turn and carefully lower it to the mat.
8   Rest, breathing regularly.

## VARIATION 3

1   Follow steps 1 and 2 of Variation 2.
2   Keeping the legs in this position, bend the head forwards and try to touch the chest with the chin. Keep the shoulders as relaxed as possible.
3   Hold the position, breathing as deeply as comfort permits, for a few seconds.
4   Release the hold on each leg in turn and carefully lower it to the floor. Relax, breathing normally.

## NOTE

If you feel more comfortable maintaining the hold on the bent leg or legs by placing your hands underneath rather than over them, please do so.

asanas

83

# THE FISH

**CAUTION** Avoid this posture if you have an abdominal hernia or neck pain, or if you suffer from vertigo, dizziness or balance disorders. Also avoid it during the first three days of menstruation, and check with your doctor if you have a thyroid gland problem and are considering practising it.

**WHAT IT DOES** The Fish posture is a splendid posture for those who suffer from asthma and other respiratory conditions. Through internal massage and stretching of the mid-trunk, it also contributes to the health of organs within your abdomen and pelvis, and is effective against constipation.

## HOW TO DO IT

**1** Lie on your back with your legs stretched out in front and your arms beside you.

**2** Bend your arms, push down on your elbows and raise your chest off the mat as you arch your back.

**3** Carefully stretch your neck and ease your head towards your shoulders; rest the top of your head on the mat. Adjust your position so that most of your weight is taken by your bottom and elbows rather than your head and neck.

**4** Hold this position for a few seconds to begin with, breathing slowly and as deeply as possible. Hold the posture longer when you feel more comfortable in it.

**5** Slowly and carefully resume your starting position. Rest.

complete yoga

# THE PELVIC TILT

**WHAT IT DOES** The Pelvic Tilt is an excellent posture for strengthening the lower back, and toning and strengthening the abdominal muscles.

## HOW TO DO IT

**1** Lie on your back, with your legs stretched out in front. Relax your jaw and breathe regularly.

**2** Slide your hands under your waist: you will note a hollow there. This is the lumbar arch of your spine.

**3** Relax your arms and hands at your sides. Bend your legs and rest the soles of your feet flat on the mat, at a comfortable distance from your bottom.

**4** Exhale and press the small of your back (waist level) towards or against the mat, to reduce or eliminate the hollow you felt there. As you do so, you will feel your pelvis tilt gently upwards.

**5** Maintain the downward pressure of your waist as long as your exhalation lasts.

**6** Inhale and relax. Breathe regularly. Repeat steps 4 to 6 once more.

**7** Stretch out your legs and rest. Breathe regularly. You may repeat the exercise later.

### NOTE

The above exercise is very good preparation for the one to follow. For maximum benefit, try doing the two in sequence.

asanas

85

# THE BRIDGE

**WHAT IT DOES**   Excellent for toning the back and abdominal muscles, the Bridge also helps to keep your spine flexible and it gives your body an all-over therapeutic stretch.

## HOW TO DO IT

1   Lie on your back, with your legs stretched out in front of you and your arms relaxed at your sides. Breathe regularly.

2   Bend your legs and rest the soles of your feet flat on the mat, at a comfortable distance from your bottom. Turn your palms down.

3   Inhaling, raise first your hips, then slowly and smoothly the rest of your back until your torso is fully raised and level. Keep your arms and hands pressed to the mat.

4   Hold the posture for as long as you are comfortable in it. Keep breathing regularly.

5   Slowly and smoothly lower your torso, from top to bottom, until it is again flat on the mat. Stretch out your legs. Turn your palms up. Rest.

# LEGS UP

This exercise is a good way to relieve tired, swollen feet. Also, by helping the return flow of blood from the legs to the heart, and lessening the wear and tear on the valves (which prevent a back-flow of blood) of the large blood vessels, it is wonderful for discouraging the formation or worsening of varicose veins. The Legs Up exercise is also a good way to promote all-over relaxation if combined with slow rhythmical breathing.

## HOW TO DO IT

1 Lie facing a wall. Lift your legs and rest them against the wall so that they form about a 45 degree angle with the mat on which you are lying.

2 Relax your arms at your sides, close your eyes and breathe slowly and regularly.

3 When you are ready to get up, do so slowly and carefully; bring your knees towards your abdomen, roll onto your side and come into a sitting position.

### VARIATION

If you feel comfortable, try taking yourself much closer to the wall so that your legs are at a 90 degree angle.

asanas

87

# THE CROCODILE

**WHAT IT DOES**   This posture is similar to the Pose of Tranquillity and promotes the same deep relaxation.

## HOW TO DO IT

**1** Lie on your abdomen, with your legs fully stretched out and comfortably separated. (You may place a thin pillow or cushion under your hips.)

**2** Fold your arms and rest your head on them. Close your eyes. Breathe regularly.

**3** Mentally go over your body, concentrating on one part at a time, giving each part silent suggestion to let go of tension and to relax completely. Include the feet, legs, hips, upper back, abdomen, chest, arms and hands, neck, head and facial muscles.

**4** If your thoughts stray, gently guide them back and continue the exercise.

**5** Finish with several minutes of slow rhythmical breathing, letting your body sink more fully onto your mat with each exhalation.

**6** Roll onto your side and use your hands to help you up.

# ALTERNATE LEG STRETCH

**WHAT IT DOES** The Alternate Leg Stretch gives natural traction to the spine, which releases pressure on nerves and discs. It therapeutically stretches and tones the back muscles. It also tones and firms the arm and leg muscles and exercises the shoulder and hip joints.

## HOW TO DO IT

**1** Sit tall with your legs stretched out in front. Breathe regularly.

**2** Fold your left leg inwards and rest the sole of the foot against the right upper thigh.

**3** Stretch out your arms and reach for your lower right leg. Exhaling, bend forwards at your hip joints (not at the waist), and hold onto your outstretched leg. Bend your elbows, lower your head and relax in the posture.

**4** Come out of the posture in reverse, synchronizing movement with regular breathing.

**5** Stretch out your folded leg and rest.

**6** Fold your right leg inwards and repeat the exercise (steps 3 to 5), substituting the word 'left' for 'right' and vice versa in the instructions.

asanas

89

# FORWARD BEND (SITTING)

**CAUTION**   Do not practise this posture if you have a hernia or a disorder of the liver, spleen or appendix. It is a deceptively simple-looking posture (as is the standing version) and so is best avoided by beginners until you have progressed in your practice.

**WHAT IT DOES**   The Forward Bend (Sitting) provides gentle traction of the spine, which releases pressure on spinal nerves and discs. It stretches and conditions the back muscles to maintain their effectiveness as spinal supports. In addition, this posture helps to prevent the hamstring muscles from shortening, and is therefore useful in the management of backache. It also promotes the health of organs within the pelvis and abdomen and helps to keep your hip and shoulder joints flexible.

## HOW TO DO IT

1   Sit tall, with your legs stretched out and together. Breathe regularly.

2   Inhale and raise your arms overhead.

3   Exhale and bend forwards, at your hip joints rather than at your waist, keeping your upper body erect. Reach for your feet.

complete yoga

4   When you can bend no further, hold on to your legs, ankles or feet. Bend your elbows to help to secure your position. Lower your head and relax in the posture, breathing regularly.

5   Stay in this posture for as long as you are comfortable in it.

6   Come out of the posture in reverse, synchronizing movement with breathing. Rest.

## VARIATION 1

Follow steps 1 to 3 of the basic exercise. Bend your ankles so that your toes point upwards. Hold on to your big toes. Bend your elbows to help you to intensify the forward bend. Lower your head and maintain the posture while breathing regularly. Come out of the posture in reverse. Rest.

## VARIATION 2

After completing your forward bend, as in step 4 of the basic posture, relax your arms and hands on the mat beside you, rather than hold on to the legs or feet.

# FORWARD BEND (STANDING)

**CAUTION**  Do not practise this posture during the first three days of menstruation. Do not practise it if you suffer from high blood pressure or any condition that produces feelings of light-headedness or dizziness when you bend down. See also cautions for the Forward Bend (Sitting).

**WHAT IT DOES**  The Forward Bend (Standing) improves the tone of the abdominal and pelvic organs through a two-fold action, namely, increasing intra-abdominal pressure and stretching the back muscles. In addition, it helps to prevent the hamstring muscles (at the back of the legs) from shortening, and is therefore useful in the management of backache. This posture is also of value for combating constipation.

## HOW TO DO IT

1  Stand tall but not rigid, with your feet close together and your arms relaxed at your sides. Breathe regularly.

2  Inhale and raise your arms overhead.

3  Exhale and bend forwards, at your hips rather than at your waist. Do not bend your knees.

4  Hold on to your lower legs or ankles. Bend your elbows and gently pull your upper body towards your legs. Avoid exerting too much pressure on your abdomen.

5  Hold the posture for as long as you comfortably can, breathing regularly but not deeply.

6  Come up slowly and carefully while inhaling. Rest.

# SPREAD LEG STRETCH

**WHAT IT DOES** The Spread Leg Stretch brings a good supply of blood to your perineal area (the lowest part of your torso), and thus contributes to the health of your pelvis. It tones and firms your inner thigh muscles and improves circulation in your legs. It also helps to keep your spine flexible and relieves pressure on spinal nerves. Diligent practice of this exercise will also contribute to relief from menstrual cramps and backache.

## HOW TO DO IT

1 Sit naturally upright on your mat, with your legs spread as far apart as is comfortable. Place your hands on your legs.

2 Exhale and bend forwards, at your hip joints rather than at your waist; keep your torso straight. Slide your hands towards your feet.

3 When you can bend no further, hold the position as long as you are comfortable in it. Keep breathing regularly.

4 Inhale and slowly resume your starting position. Rest.

asanas

93

# POSE OF A CHILD

**WHAT IT DOES**     This posture, regularly practised, helps keep your spine flexible. As you breathe rhythmically while in this position, your internal organs receive a gentle, therapeutic massage which promotes circulation and facilitates elimination. It is also a very relaxing posture and an excellent one following backward-bending postures such as The Cobra and The Locust.

## HOW TO DO IT

1 Sit on your heels, Japanese style. Breathe regularly.

2 Bend forwards slowly, resting your forehead on the mat or turning your face to the side. Relax your arms and hands beside you.

3 Stay in this position for as long as you feel comfortable in it. Keep breathing regularly.

4 Slowly resume your starting position.

### NOTE

If you cannot get your head down onto the mat, place a cushion or pillow in front of you and rest your forehead or cheek on it.

### VARIATION

Follow steps 1 and 2 of the instructions for the basic posture, but modify step 2 so that you stretch your arms straight out in front of you instead of resting them beside you.

complete yoga

# TRIANGLE POSTURE

**WHAT IT DOES** For suppleness and elasticity, the Triangle Posture provides therapeutic stretching of various ordinarily under-exercised muscles. It tones the muscles of your back and abdomen and improves muscular support for the organs within your abdomen and pelvis. It offers gentle, effective stretching for the muscles of your legs and arms.

## HOW TO DO IT

1 Stand erect, with your feet together and your arms at your sides. Breathe regularly.

2 Exhaling, bend forwards at your hips rather than at your waist. Keep your upper body and legs straight.

3 Try to touch your toes with your fingertips. Do not lower your head; keep it aligned with your back.

4 Hold the position for as long as you comfortably can, breathing regularly.

5 Inhale and resume your starting position.

# THE PLOUGH

**CAUTION**    Do not practise The Plough during the first few days of menstruation. Avoid it also if you have a uterine prolapse or a hernia, or if you suffer from neck pain or spinal disc problems. In any event, check with your doctor before practising The Plough. If you do practise the exercise, be especially carefully not to exert unnecessary pressure on your neck. Do not let your buttocks go beyond your shoulders, as this can place too much strain on your neck.

**WHAT IT DOES**    Studies in India indicate that regular practice of The Plough can lengthen the spine, in some cases by nearly 15 per cent. When this occurs, the vertebral foramina (openings), through which the spinal nerves pass, are enlarged, and pressure on these nerves is eased. (Faulty postures during day-to-day activities result in such pressure.) This improves the circulation in your spinal cord (which is an extension of your brain), and thus also the functioning of internal organs supplied by these nerves.

The Plough is also effective in preventing an accumulation of toxic substances in the body. The contraction of the abdominal muscles and the hips-high, head-low position helps drain internal structures and strengthen them. Wastes are effectively eliminated and your body becomes healthier and your mind clearer.

## HOW TO DO IT

1   Lie on your back, with your arms stretched out at your sides and the palms of your hands turned down. Breathe regularly.

2   Bring your knees to your chest, then straighten your legs so that your feet point up. (Do not raise both legs up at the same time from a lying position, as you may hurt your back.)

complete yoga

3 On an exhalation, kick backwards with both feet at once until your hips are raised. Push your feet towards the mat behind your head. Keep your legs straight and together if possible.

4 Hold the completed position for as long as you can with absolute comfort. Breathe regularly.

5 To resume your starting position, slowly, smoothly and carefully roll your spine onto the mat; bend your legs and stretch them out. Rest.

NOTE
_____

Do not be discouraged if your toes do not immediately touch the mat. They will, eventually, as your spine becomes flexible. In the meantime, you can try putting a few cushions behind you so that your feet can touch something. This will serve as a guide to your progress.

asanas

97

# PELVIC STRETCH

**WHAT IT DOES** The Pelvic Stretch gives a therapeutic stretch to your groin, and improves circulation in the entire pelvic region. This benefits all pelvic structures.

## HOW TO DO IT

1 Sit on your heels Japanese style.

2 Put your hands on the mat behind your feet, fingers pointing back. Breathe regularly.

3 Inhaling, carefully tilt your head slightly backwards. Press on your palms and raise your bottom off your heels, as high as you comfortably can.

4 Maintain this position for as long as is comfortable, breathing regularly.

5 Slowly ease yourself back into your starting position.

### NOTE

A good way to rest following this posture is in the Pose of a Child (page 94).

# THE CAMEL

**CAUTION** Avoid this posture if you suffer from neck pains or spinal disc problems, or if you have a hernia.

**WHAT IT DOES** The Camel strengthens your back and keeps your spine flexible. It has a beneficial influence on your endocrine glands (such as the thyroid and the ovaries). It strengthens the urinary and reproductive organs, and conditions your hip and thigh muscles.

## HOW TO DO IT

1 Kneel down with your legs together and your toes pointing backwards.

2 Support the small of your back (waist level) with your hands, and very carefully tilt your head back.

3 Slowly and carefully place your right hand on your right heel and your left hand on your left heel. Keep your hips high.

4 Hold this position for as long as you can with absolute comfort, breathing regularly.

NOTE

In due course, you may be interested in a more challenging version of this exercise: rest your hands on the mat behind your feet rather than on your heels.

5 Very slowly and carefully resume your starting position. Rest in the Pose of a Child (page 94).

# THE COBRA

**CAUTION**  Do not include The Cobra in your exercise programme if you have a hernia.

**WHAT IT DOES**  The Cobra is excellent for promoting and maintaining the elasticity of your spine. It enhances spinal circulation and relieves the pressure on nerves branching off the spine – often a result of bad postural habits. This position also exercises the joints of your shoulders, elbows and wrists and so helps keep them flexible.

## HOW TO DO IT

**1** Lie on your abdomen, with your head turned to the side. Relax your arms and hands beside you. Breathe regularly.

**2** Turn your head to the front, resting your forehead on the mat. Place your palms on the mat, directly beneath your shoulders. Keep your arms close to your sides.

**3** As you inhale, bend backwards slowly and carefully; touch the mat with your nose then your chin, in one smooth movement. Breathe regularly and continue arching the rest of your spine – your upper back then your lower back, in one slow, smooth, graceful movement. Keep your hips in contact with the mat throughout the exercise.

**4** When you can arch your back no further, hold the position but do not hold your breath. Keep breathing regularly.

**5** When you are ready to come out of the position, do so in reverse very slowly, smoothly and with control; lower your abdomen to the mat; lower your chest, chin, nose and forehead, in synchronization with regular breathing.

**6** Relax your arms and hands beside you. Turn your head to the side. Rest.

complete yoga

# HALF LOCUST

**CAUTION** Avoid the Half Locust if you have a serious heart condition or a hernia.

**WHAT IT DOES** Excellent for strengthening your back and your legs, the Half Locust – through gentle yet effective internal massage – improves the function of the kidneys and adrenal glands, and also helps to counteract constipation.

## HOW TO DO IT

**1** Lie on your abdomen with your chin on the mat and your legs close together. Straighten your arms and position them, close together, under your body. Make fists and keep your thumbs down. (Alternatively, keep your arms by your body.) Breathe regularly.

**2** Exhale and slowly and carefully raise one still-straight leg as high as you comfortably can. Keep your chin, arms and body pressed to the mat.

**3** Hold the raised-leg posture as long as you comfortably can, breathing regularly.

**4** Lower your leg to the mat, slowly and with control. Rest.

**5** Repeat the exercise with your other leg. You may rest in the Pose of a Child (page 94).

asanas

101

# THE BOW

**CAUTION**     Avoid this exercise if you have a serious heart condition or a hernia.

**WHAT IT DOES**     The Bow keeps your spine flexible and strengthens your back and abdominal muscles. Through gentle but effective massage, it improves the functioning of organs and glands in the kidney area, as well as those within the abdomen. It helps to counteract constipation, and expands the chest to facilitate deep breathing for the better nourishment of all body tissues.

## HOW TO DO IT

1 Lie face down, with your legs comfortably separated and your arms beside you. Breathe regularly.

2 Bend your knees and bring your feet close to your bottom.

3 Carefully tilt your head back; reach for your feet and grasp your ankles. Keep breathing regularly.

4 Exhaling, push your feet upwards and away from you. This action will raise your legs and arch your body.

5 Breathing regularly, hold the position for as long as you comfortably can.

6 Resume your starting position. Push yourself up onto your hands and knees and relax in the Pose of a Child (page 94).

complete yoga

# INCLINED PLANE

**WHAT IT DOES** The Inclined Plane gives a wonderful top-to-toe stretch and is excellent for strengthening your arms, legs and torso.

## HOW TO DO IT

1   Sit tall, with your legs together and stretched out in front. Rest your hands on the mat behind you, with your fingers pointing away from you. Breathe regularly.

2   Press on your palms to help you raise your body. Hold your hips high. Carefully tilt your head back. Your weight should be borne by your palms and feet (or heels).

3   Hold the posture for as long as you are comfortable in it, breathing regularly.

4   Lower your body to the mat and go back to your starting position. Relax your arms and hands. Rest.

### NOTE

This posture requires strength in the arms, wrists, ankles and legs. If you find it hard or impossible to do at first, persevere with exercises such as The Flower (page 69), warm-ups for the hand, wrists and ankles (Chapter 4), and postures such as the Chest Expander (page 78) and the standing balances like the Balance Posture (page 76) for a period of time until you have acquired the necessary stamina. Do not strain.

asanas

# SIDE LEG RAISE

This exercise tones the muscles of your inner thighs and improves circulation to your lower pelvis. It also discourages a build-up of fatty deposits around your waist.

## HOW TO DO IT

1 Lie on your side, supporting your head with your hand. You may bend your lower leg slightly. Rest the palm of your opposite hand on the floor in front of you, for stability.

2 Inhale and slowly raise your upper leg, trying to keep it directly over the lower one, rather than behind or in front of it. Keep your raised leg as straight as you can.

3 Hold this position as long as you comfortably can, breathing regularly.

4 Exhale and lower your leg. Rest.

5 Repeat the exercise, lying on the other side this time.

# HALF MOON

**WHAT IT DOES**   The Half Moon provides sideways (lateral) bending of your torso, thus contributing to the health of your spine. It helps keep your shoulder joints flexible and exercises the midriff to discourage a build-up of fat. It also enhances breathing.

## HOW TO DO IT

1   Stand naturally erect, with your feet close together and your body weight equally distributed between them. Relax your arms at your sides. Breathe regularly.

2   Inhale and bring your arms up. Press your palms together if you can. Keep your arms alongside your ears.

3   Exhale, and slowly and smoothly bend to one side to form a graceful arch.

4   Hold this position for as long as you comfortably can, breathing regularly.

5   Inhale and return to the upright position. Exhale and lower your arms.

6   Repeat steps 2 to 5, bending to the other side. Rest.

asanas

105

# ANGLE POSTURE

**WHAT IT DOES** Used as a complement to the Triangle Posture (page 95), this exercise is excellent for stretching and toning the lateral (side) muscles of your trunk and for discouraging a build-up of fat around your waist. It also improves abdominal and pelvic circulation.

## HOW TO DO IT

1 Stand erect, with your arms at your sides and your feet about 60 centimetres (24 inches) apart. Breathe regularly.

2 Inhaling, raise your left arm; exhale and bend sideways to the right, sliding your right hand down the side of your right leg. Keep your left arm alongside your ear.

3 When you can bend no further, hold the position for as long as you are comfortable in it. Continue breathing regularly.

4 Inhale and return to the upright position; exhale and lower your arm.

5 Repeat the sideways bend to the other side (substitute the word 'right' for 'left' and vice versa in the instructions).

complete yoga

# SPINAL TWIST

This is the only yoga posture that requires maximum torsion (twisting) of the spine; first to one side, then to the other, causing the vertebrae to rotate one over the other and to bend at the same time to the right or left. This spinal action gives a therapeutic massage to nerves branching off the spinal column. Muscles of the lower back are also stretched and contracted during this exercise. This enhances the blood circulation in the area of your kidneys and revitalizes your adrenal glands.

## HOW TO DO IT

1 Sit naturally erect on your mat, with your legs stretched out in front of you. Breathe regularly.

2 Bend your right leg at the knee and place your right foot beside your left knee. Keep breathing regularly.

3 On an exhalation, slowly and smoothly twist your upper body to the right, placing one or both hands on the mat at your right side. Turn your head and look over your right shoulder.

4 Hold this position as long as you comfortably can, continuing to breathe regularly.

5 Slowly and smoothly untwist and resume your starting position.

6 Repeat steps 2 to 5 in the opposite direction (substitute the word 'left' for 'right' and vice versa in the instructions). Rest.

### VARIATION

To enhance the benefits of this posture, place the foot of the bent leg on the outside of the straight leg. This increases the stretch.

asanas

107

# CROSS BEAM

The Cross Beam stretches the body sideways, thereby contributing to the health of the spine. It conditions the back and abdominal muscles, and discourages a build-up of fat around the midriff. It also tones and firms the muscles of the arms and legs.

## HOW TO DO IT

1 Kneel on your mat. Breathe regularly.

2 Stretch your right leg out to the side; point your toes towards the front rather than sideways, to prevent you from going into a 'split' as you do the posture.

3 Rest your right arm on your outstretched leg; turn your palm up.

4 Exhale and bend to the right, aiming your right ear towards your right leg. Raise your left arm and bring it towards your right leg. As you do so, your right arm will slide down the leg. Keep your left shoulder back to ensure a side rather than a forward bend.

5 Hold the posture for as long as you are comfortable in it, breathing regularly. Slowly and carefully return to your starting position, as in step 1. Repeat.

6 Repeat steps 2 to 6 on the other side (substitute the word 'left' for 'right' and vice versa in the instructions).

# DOG STRETCH

**CAUTION** Omit the Dog Stretch if you suffer from high blood pressure or have a heart condition, or any disorder that produces feelings of light-headedness or dizziness when you hang your head down. See also the Half Shoulderstand (page 110) for other cautions related to inverted postures.

**WHAT IT DOES** This exercise is wonderful for helping to maintain the elasticity of the hamstring muscles at the back of your legs. When the hamstrings shorten, they adversely affect the tilt of your pelvis and may thus contribute to backache. It also relaxes tired legs and can help the entire body.

## HOW TO DO IT

1 Start in an 'all fours' position on your hands and knees. Let your arms slope forwards. Breathe regularly.

2 Tuck your toes in so that they point forwards. Rock backwards slightly. Raise your knees and straighten your legs. Straighten your arms. Look down. You are now in a hips-high, head-low position. Aim your heels towards the mat but do not strain the muscles at the back of your legs.

3 Stay in this posture for as long as you are comfortable in it, breathing regularly.

4 Rock forward gently before returning to your starting position. Sit on your heels, with your toes pointing back.

5 Rest in the Pose of a Child (page 94).

asanas

109

# HALF SHOULDERSTAND

**CAUTION** Avoid this and other inverted postures if you have an ear or eye disorder, or if you suffer from heart disease, high blood pressure or other circulatory disorders. Do not practise inverted postures during menstruation. In any event, check with your doctor before attempting the Half Shoulderstand and other head-low hips-high postures.

**WHAT IT DOES** The health-giving benefits of this inverted posture are the result of the stretching and contraction of three muscle groups: your back muscles, which are stretched; your abdominal muscles, which are contracted; and the muscles at the front of your neck, which are also contracted. The organs within your trunk are also revitalized, improving blood circulation and the function of the lymphatic, endocrine and nervous systems. In addition, by summoning the aid of gravitational forces, this inverted posture greatly benefits the health of your skin and hair. It facilitates circulation to the upper body, enriching tissues such as those of your face and scalp.

## HOW TO DO IT

1 Lie on your back on a mat. Bend your knees and rest the soles of your feet flat on the mat. Keep your arms close to your sides. Breathe regularly throughout the exercise.

2 Bring first one knee, then the other, to your chest.

3 Straighten one leg at a time until your feet point up.

4 Kick backwards with both feet at once, until your hips are off the mat. Support your hips with your hands, thumbs in front.

complete yoga

**5** Maintain this position for a few seconds to begin with; longer as you become more comfortable with it.

**6** To come out of the posture, place your hands on the mat again, close to your body.

**7** Keep your head firmly pressed to the mat (perhaps tilting your chin slightly upwards), and slowly and carefully lower your torso, from top to bottom, onto the mat. Bend your knees and stretch out your legs, one at a time. Rest.

### NOTE

If you are unable to do the Half Shoulderstand but wish to gain some of the benefits of an inverted posture, try the Dog Stretch (page 109). Check with your doctor first.

# FULL SHOULDERSTAND

CAUTION These are the same as for the Half Shoulderstand (page 110). Avoid the Full Shoulderstand if you suffer from neck pain.

WHAT IT DOES The benefits derived from the Full Shoulderstand are the same as those of the Half Shoulderstand. In addition, it enhances thyroid gland function. The thyroid gland controls your body's metabolism, so when it is functioning well all cells and tissues benefit.

## HOW TO DO IT

1 Lie on your back on a mat. Bend your knees and rest the soles of your feet flat on the mat. Keep your arms close to your sides. Breathe regularly throughout the exercise.

2 Bring first one knee, then the other, to your chest.

3 Straighten one leg at a time until your feet point up.

4 Kick backwards with both feet at once, until your hips are off the mat. Support your hips with your hands, thumbs in front.

5 Gradually move your hands, one at a time, towards your upper back, until your body is in as vertical a position as you can manage with complete comfort. Your chin should be in contact with your chest and your body as relaxed as possible.

6 Hold the position for a few seconds to begin with, working up to two or more minutes as you become accustomed to it.

7 To come out of the posture, tilt your feet slightly backwards. Rest your arms beside your body and keep your head pressed to the mat. Slowly lower your hips to the mat. Bend your legs and lower them, one at a time, to the mat. Rest.

# MOCK HEADSTAND

If you have high blood pressure or neck pain, check with your doctor before practising this posture.

This exercise brings a fresh supply of blood to the face and the scalp, which benefits your skin and hair. It also promotes general relaxation.

## HOW TO DO IT

1 Sit on your heels, with your toes pointing backwards. Breathe regularly throughout the exercise.

2 Lean forward and rest your forehead on the mat, close to your knees.

3 Carefully raise your bottom from your heels until the top of your head rests on the mat. Do not exert pressure on your skull. Hold on to your heels or ankles.

4 Hold the position for only a few seconds at first, working up to a minute or two as you become more comfortable in it.

5 To come out of the posture, ease yourself slowly towards your heels. Keep your head low for a few seconds before gradually sitting upright on your heels. Rest before getting up.

asanas

113

# CAT STRETCH SEQUENCE

Avoid this series of exercises if you suffer from epilepsy.

The Cat Stretch series helps to keep your spine flexible. It conditions the back muscles which support your spine, and tones and firms your abdominal muscles, which complement your back muscles as spinal supports. It also provides therapeutic stretching of your legs, and improves your general circulation.

## HOW TO DO IT

1 Get on your hands and knees in an 'all fours' position.

2 Exhaling, lower your head, arch your shoulders and tuck your hips down so that your entire back is rounded.

3 Inhale and resume your starting position. Exhale.

complete yoga

114

**4** Inhaling, bend your elbows and lower your chest to the mat, taking care not to let your back sag. Keep your head back so that your neck receives a gentle stretch as your chin touches the mat. Let your arms and hands take most of the weight to avoid unnecessary pressure on your back.

**5** Exhale and return to the 'all fours' position. Breathe regularly.

**6** Exhaling, lower your head, make your back rounded and bring one knee towards your forehead.

**7** Inhaling, push your bent leg backwards, stretching it out fully and lifting it as high as you can with comfort; raise your head. Take care not to accentuate the arch in your lower back as you do this movement.

**8** Exhale and lower your knee to the mat.

**9** Repeat steps 6 and 7 with the other leg.

**10** Repeat step 8.

**11** Lie down and rest, breathing regularly, or rest in the Pose of a Child (page 94).

chapter six

# meditation

Known as Nature's tranquillizer, meditation on a regular basis provides a superb antidote to stress. It brings about well-documented physiological changes that enable the meditator to achieve a state of 'restful alertness'. You can apply meditation principles to many of your daily activities to keep you calm and focused, even when under pressure. This chapter gives prerequisites for meditating successfully, and describes simple meditation techniques.

Doctors describe the state of restful alertness that occurs in meditation as 'hypometabolic awareness'. It means that you are still awake and conscious even though your metabolism has slowed down. This meditative state has also been referred to as one of 'restful alertness', an apparent contradiction. When you are asleep, for example, your heart rate becomes slower, oxygen consumption decreases and consciousness fades. When you are awake, by contrast, your heartbeat quickens, oxygen consumption increases and you are usually alert. These opposites are united in meditation, so that although your body becomes deeply relaxed, you are conscious and your mind remains clear.

Meditation, then, is a process for quieting the mind. When your mind is quiet, you feel peaceful.

## BENEFITS

An athlete tunes and trains his or her body. Meditation tunes and trains the mind. The end result is efficiency in everyday living. To have any real and lasting value, however, meditation must be consistently repeated over time. Meditating regularly helps you to bring deep-seated tensions to the surface and to cope with them. Consequently, you become more at ease with yourself and comfortable with others. This results in greater self-confidence and enhanced productivity. You gain a greater sense of self-control so that you feel less at the mercy of outside forces. As a result, things which you may have perceived as insurmountable in the past begin to appear at least manageable. In a nutshell, meditation helps to integrate and strengthen your personality, allowing you to become serene and competent.

Meditation is nature's own tranquillizer. Unlike its chemical counterparts, it enables you to go deep within yourself to the source of disturbances: to identify them, become more aware of them and acquire and exercise more control over them.

Meditation helps to keep you in the present. States such as anxiety, apprehension, worry and depression represent concerns about past and future events. When we live life with full focus on the present, even major events lose their ability to cause the distress they otherwise might. When you take care of the present, the future tends to take care of itself. When you worry unduly about the future or become preoccupied with the past, you miss what the present has to offer and you also decrease your chances of future success. It is prudent to plan for the future and it is reasonable to reflect on the past; but it is unwise to dwell in either place.

Meditation helps to keep you young. Researchers have discovered that long-term meditation helps to decrease a person's metabolic age and also to give protection against certain disorders, such as heart disease and cancer. Increasingly, doctors are recommending a period or two of daily meditation as an adjunct to treatments for conditions such as heart disease, high blood pressure, migraine headaches, stomach and intestinal ulcers and various nervous system disorders.

There is no single way of meditating that is best for everyone. Each person must find the method that is most compatible with his or her personality through experimentation. You should feel better, not worse, after meditating than you did before.

## PREPARATION

Since it is easier to gain control over the body than it is to gain control over the mind, a good place to begin is with simple stretching exercises. You will find that practising the exercises described in Chapter 5 every day or every other day can be helpful in acquiring that control.

The next preparatory step for meditation is being able to pay attention and stay focused. The exercises in Chapter 5 also train you to do this. So do the breathing techniques in Chapter 3, such as Alternate Nostril Breathing and the Whispering Breath, which encourage the 'one-pointedness' necessary for successful meditation.

Other prerequisites for meditation are as follows:

◆ The ability to sit still for up to 20 minutes at a time. A folded-legs posture, such as that depicted in the Mountain Posture (see page 66), provides a stable base for such a purpose. If you are unable to sit in this manner, or if you find it uncomfortable, any other sitting position that holds your spine in good alignment, and in which you are completely comfortable, will do. Sitting still is very important for successful meditation because the less body movement there is, the steadier the mind will be.
◆ Daily practice of the Pose of Tranquillity (see page 54) will train you in the art of total relaxation and is therefore very worthwhile.
◆ Meditate before, rather than after, a meal to prevent the process of digestion from interfering with your concentration.
◆ Meditate in a quiet place where you can remain uninterrupted for about 20 minutes.
◆ Try to meditate at least once a day but preferably twice. Start with five minutes and gradually increase meditation time to 20 minutes a session.
◆ If after practising a particular meditation several times you do not feel completely comfortable with it, discard it and try another until you find one with which you feel totally at ease.
◆ Be patient. Do not expect the desired results after meditating only a few times. Persevere. Skill and ease will come with time and repeated practice.

# BREATH AWARENESS

Breath awareness is an essential part of meditation. Most well-established schools teach it as the natural first step towards advanced meditation techniques. Beginners should therefore develop the habit of breath awareness first, rather than become unduly preoccupied with some other activity or object on which to focus their attention. The results of practising Breath Awareness every day include a decrease in tension build-up and a harmonizing of body, mind and spirit.

## HOW TO DO IT

1 Sit comfortably with your body relaxed, as described in the previous section on 'preparation'.

2 With eyes closed, focus your attention only on your breathing, without in any way manipulating it. Become, as it were, a silent observer of your own breathing process: note its rate, its depth or shallowness, its smoothness or jerkiness, its sounds or its quietness and the natural pause occurring between exhalation and inhalation.

Do not end your meditation abruptly. Sit quietly for a few minutes and assess how you feel. If the meditation is right for you, you will feel calmer and more organized (more 'together') than you did before you meditated. You will then look forward to a regular period of Breath Awareness and you will be motivated to practise it.

### NOTES

The object is to keep your attention on the breathing cycle and to observe it. Start with a few minutes and increase the time as you become more familiar and comfortable with the exercise.

# CANDLE CONCENTRATION

**WHAT IT DOES** Candle Concentration promotes relaxation and is a good pre-sleep exercise for those who suffer from insomnia. It improves concentration and also helps improve or correct certain eye weaknesses.

## HOW TO DO IT

Place a lighted candle at (or slightly below) eye level, on a table, stool or other appropriate place.

1 Sit naturally erect and breathe regularly. Look intently at the candle flame. Blink if necessary.

2 Now close your eyes and retain or recall the image of the flame. Do not be anxious if it disappears. Try to recall the image and fix your attention on it. Keep breathing regularly.

3 After about two minutes open your eyes. As you become more comfortable with the technique, lengthen practice time to five or ten minutes.

Do not end your meditation abruptly. Sit quietly for a few minutes and assess how you feel. If the meditation is right for you, you will feel calmer and more organized.

meditation

121

# A SIMPLE MEDITATION

WHAT IT DOES This exercise calms the mind and is particularly useful when you are faced with a challenging or perplexing situation. It provides you with a focal point which will help you to maintain a certain detachment and give you a measure of control. It will also help you to re-establish you equilibrium.

## HOW TO DO IT

1 Sit comfortably. Close your eyes. Relax your body. Breathe regularly.

2 Inhale slowly and smoothly through your nostrils.

3 As you exhale slowly and smoothly through your nostrils, mentally say the word 'one'. Repeat steps 2 and 3 again and again in smooth succession.

If your thoughts stray, guide them back patiently to both the breathing and the repetition of 'one'. Do not be discouraged if this occurs frequently at first. With regular practice, your ability to remain one-pointed will improve.

When you are ready to end your period of meditation, do so slowly: open your eyes and gently stretch and/or massage your limbs. Never come out of meditation suddenly.

### NOTES

You may substitute any word or short phrase for 'one'. Particularly effective is something related to your religion. Other suggestions are 'peace', 'calm', 'relax', 'I feel calm', 'love and light' and 'nothing can harm me'.

complete yoga

# SERENITY: A VISUALIZATION

WHAT IT DOES As with all meditation practices, this visualization exercise calms the mind. It is a very apt exercise to recall in troubled times, as it will restore a sense of balance.

## HOW TO DO IT

1 Sit or lie in any comfortable position, with your spine in good alignment. Close your eyes. Relax your jaw. Breathe regularly.

2 Relax your body from top to toe, using the Pose of Tranquillity (page 54) as a guide.

3 Imagine lying or sitting beside a beautiful lake. No ripples disturb its surface; it is perfectly still. Imagine your mind becoming as tranquil as the lake, which is vast. Capture the sense of spaciousness. The lake is also crystal-clear. Visualize your mind becoming equally clear. The lake is untroubled. Visualize your mind similarly carefree and tranquil.

4 The sun sends its comforting rays upon the lake. Sense this warmth upon your body and a feeling of peace enfolding you.

5 Shift your focus of attention to your breathing: with each incoming breath absorb those properties attributed to the sun — light, warmth and energy; with each outgoing breath, let your body sink a little more deeply into the surface on which you are lying or sitting. Give up any residual tensions your body may be harbouring. Totally surrender yourself to the serenity of your environment.

Stay with this image for about five minutes to begin with. Increase the time as you become more practised and comfortable with the visualization

meditation

123

chapter seven

# yoga in pregnancy

This chapter features more than a dozen exercises to tone and stretch the muscles that will be involved in childbirth. With your doctor's permission, practise them daily. Along with some of the breathing exercises in chapter 3 and meditation techniques in chapter 6, you now have tools to confidently prepare yourself for your child's arrival. And with your doctor's permission also, you can quickly regain figure and function with the postnatal exercises at the end of the chapter.

Pregnancy is not an illness but a natural function. Although there was a time when a pregnant woman was thought to be in a 'delicate state' and encouraged to do as little as possible, pregnancy is now considered a time when a woman should be at her fittest so as to meet the increased demands made of her not only physically, but also mentally and emotionally. This makes yoga perfect for the pregnant woman.

It is generally accepted that a woman can better approach childbirth calmly and with confidence if her muscles are toned and she has learned how to control them; if she has understood breath control; if she has taught herself how to relax completely at will; and if she has taken nutritional and other measures to maintain good general health. Postnatally, the woman who has followed a regime of suitable exercise, coupled with correct breathing during her pregnancy will find that as she continues her exercises she very quickly recovers her strength (providing that everything has followed a normal course). She speedily regains her figure and in some cases acquires a better one, and is able to enjoy her family and life in general more fully.

Why is the yoga system of physical exercise so ideal for the pregnant woman? It calls for very gentle, rhythmic movements, and emphasizes that one should never strain or push oneself beyond one's comfortable limit. It also stresses proper breathing and draws attention to the many benefits of complete relaxation.

As mentioned earlier, the postures are designed to tone and strengthen not only the skeletal muscles, but also the glands and organs of the body, thereby generally improving the blood circulation and the functioning of the entire organism. The folded leg postures (eg. Perfect Posture) help to improve the flexibility of the hip joints, relax the muscles of the pelvic floor and encourage a feeling of openess. This is why yoga is so suitable for the pregnant woman; no strain whatever is involved if correctly applied, and fatigue is not allowed to accumulate.

In recent years there has been growing appreciation and acceptance in medical and related circles of the interdependence of body, mind and emotions. Yoga postures benefit all these simultaneously, promoting physical fitness, sound nerves and a calmer personality. The influence of the mind and emotions on childbirth is profound, as many doctors and scientists will attest.

When I was studying obstetrics, we, the students, were required to perform antenatal exercises and breathing patterns based on the psychoprophylaxis method of childbirth preparation. Participating in these exercises provided us with better insight, understanding and patience to help women in labour. Later, when I began to practise Hatha Yoga (physical yoga) I was amazed at the similarity between many of the asanas (postures) and the antenatal exercises we had learned. I subsequently discovered that some authorities claim that the psychoprophylaxis techniques are largely based on yoga which is many thousands of years old. It appeared to me that the yoga method was, in actual fact, ideal for the pregnant woman. It is gentle, rhythmic and non-fatiguing, working not only on muscles to improve their tone, but also on the nervous system, and through the breath to stablilize the emotions. In short, yoga seemed to me to meet more fully the needs of the pregnant woman, whether these needs be physical, mental or emotional.

During pregnancy the body is subject to many additional stresses and strains – a larger volume of circulating blood, harder work for the heart, greater weight for the skeletal and other muscles to support, a greater tendency to emotional upsets, and more susceptibility to tension and therefore fatigue. It is thus essential, not only to the welfare of the woman but also to that of the unborn child, that the body be kept superbly fit and beautifully relaxed. The woman should learn how to conserve energy and forestall fatigue before it accumulates to any significant degree. How indispensable and how very welcome are good muscle tone, a plentiful reserve of energy, a calm attitude, the ability to relax adequately at will, and the capacity to cooperate fully with obstetrical attendants as they instruct you in suitable breathing and other comfort measures during labour! Yoga can help you achieve all this.

Make the most of your pregnancy. It can be a very fruitful time – a time for character building and a time for cultivating healthy habits which can be of tremendous benefit, not only to you, but through you to your family.

## GENERAL CAUTIONS

Before attempting to do any of the exercises in this chapter (indeed in the rest of the book), be sure to check with your doctor. If you have a history of actual or threatened miscarriage, do not do the exercises in the first three or four months of pregnancy.

If you have venous blood clots or varicose veins, omit the folded-legs postures (such as The Perfect Posture on page 135) and the Firm Posture on page 136.

Do not practise lying postures in the prone (face downward) position, such as The Cobra (page 100), the Half Locust (page 101) and The Bow (page 102).

Please also review the general cautions in chapter 2.

## ANTENATAL SEQUENCE

| | |
|---|---|
| Warm-ups | Figure of Eight (page 40), Shoulder rotations (page 42), The Butterfly (page 129), The Cat Pose (pages 140–141): repeat steps 2 to 4 a few times in smooth succession, before resting. |
| Backward-bending postures | The Pelvic Tilt (page 144) followed by The Bridge (page 145). |
| Forward-bending postures | The Knee Press (page 142) and any of its variations (page 143) |
| Sideways-stretching posture | Sideways Swing (page 148) |
| Twisting posture | Spinal Twist (Simplified) (page 146) |
| Perineal exercise (to strengthen and tone the pelvic floor) | In any comfortable position (lying, sitting, squatting or standing), tighten your perineum (lowest part of your torso, between the external genitals and the anus) on an exhalation. Hold the tightness as long as your exhalation lasts. Release the tightness as you breathe regularly. Repeat the exercise periodically during the day. |
| Relaxation | Pose of Traquillity (page 54) |
| Breathing exercise | Diaphragmatic Breathing (page 25) |
| Meditative exercise | A Simple Meditation (page 122) for at least 5 minutes |

# THE BUTTERFLY

Avoid sitting in this posture if you experience any pain in your pubic area.

The Butterfly loosens the ankle, knee and hip joints. It also stretches and tones the adductor muscles running along the inner thighs.

## HOW TO DO IT

1 Sit with the legs outstretched in front and comfortably separated. You may place your hands on the floor beside you for support and balance.

2 Bend the right leg (you may use your hands to help), bringing the sole of the foot opposite the left thigh, and letting the knee fall outwards.

3 Bend the left leg as you did the right and place the sole of the left foot against the sole of the right one.

4 Keeping the body erect but not rigid, and relaxing the facial muscles, hold the feet together by clasping the hands around them. Take a few slow, deep breaths and then pull the feet as close to the pubic area as comfortable. Alternatively, pull the feet close to you and then place the hands on the floor behind the hips, finger pointing away from you. Straighten arms and spine. When the abdomen is quite large, this may prove more convenient.

5 Gently lower and raise the knees in a sort of flapping motion. Repeat the movements several times, incorporating a comfortable breathing rhythm.

6 Relax, breathing normally.

# THE RAISED LEG POSTURE (ALTERNATE LEG RAISE)

**WHAT IT DOES** This posture limbers, strengthens and tones the ankles and legs. It also warms, strengthens and tones the muscles of the back and abdomen.

## HOW TO DO IT

**1** Lie on your back with the legs outstretched in front and fairly close together. Arms are relaxed alongside the body, with the palms turned down.

**2** Press the small of the back against the mat to reduce the spinal arch there — this protects the back and abdominal muscles from strain and helps control the leg movements to follow. Your knees may bend slightly as you do this, but this is perfectly all right if comfortable.

**3** Locking the right knee, that is, keeping it straight, pull the toes towards you as you simultaneously push the heel away from you. With the leg in this position you are now ready to raise it. Keep the left leg relaxed.

**4** Slowly raise the right leg off the mat. Some people find it easier to exhale as the leg is raised; others prefer to inhale. Experiment to find what is more comfortable for you. When you have raised the leg as far as comfort permits, hold the position for a few seconds, breathing as normally as possible.

**5** Slowly and carefully lower the leg, inhaling or exhaling as preferred. Relax, breathing normally.

**6** Repeat steps 2 to 5, raising the left leg this time, and keeping the right one relaxed on the mat.

## VARIATION 1

1  Lie down as described in step 1. Bend the right leg at the knee and bring it towards the chest, allowing it to fall slightly outward rather than directly onto the abdomen. Do this on an exhalation.
2  Slowly and carefully straighten the leg as you inhale. Hold this position, breathing normally.
3  Bend the leg at the knee as you exhale, and lower it to the floor as you inhale. Relax, breathing normally.
4  Repeat steps 1 to 3, raising the left leg this time.
5  Perform these movements about three times with each leg.

## VARIATION 2

1  Lie down as described in step 1.
2  Bend the right leg just enough to place the sole of the foot flat on the floor.
3  Slowly and carefully raise the left leg, incorporating rhythmical breathing. Hold the raised leg position for a few seconds, breathing as normally as possible. Lower the leg carefully. Relax. Repeat twice. Relax.
4  Repeat steps 2 and 3, raising the right leg this time.

yoga in pregnancy

# THE DISCIPLE (OR STUDENT) POSTURE

**CAUTION** Avoid sitting in this posture if you experience any pain in your pubic area.

## HOW TO DO IT

1 Sit comfortably erect with the legs outstretched in front of you. To begin with, you may place your hands on the floor beside or behind you for support.

2 Bend your right leg at the knee, and with the help of your hands, place the sole of the foot against the inner surface of the opposite thigh. If this is too difficult, place it against the knee or other part of the leg that is easiest to reach.

3 Place your hands over respective knees or in any other comfortable position, and make sure that the whole body, facial muscles included, is at ease.

4 After a while, change the position of the legs so that right leg is outstretched and the left bent.

# THE EASY POSE
# (TAILOR SITTING)

**CAUTION** Avoid sitting in this posture if you experience any pain in your pubic area.

**WHAT IT DOES** When sitting in this pose you are said also to be sitting 'tailor fashion' because the position brings into play the sartorius or tailor muscles which lie across the thighs, from about the front of the hipbones to what we know as the shinbones. These muscles are the ones used in bending the legs and turning them inward, movements which will be involved in this pose.

## HOW TO DO IT: PART 1

1 Sit comfortably erect with the legs outstretched.

2 Cross the legs at the ankles and, supporting yourself with the hands on the floor beside you, draw the crossed legs close to the body, as near to the pubic area as possible. Relax the legs to permit the knees to fall outwards.

3 Sit in this position with your hands resting on your knees, or upturned, one on top of the other, on your lap. Check to see that all parts of your body not directly involved in the movements are relaxed.

## HOW TO DO IT: PART 2

**1** Sit with the legs outstretched in front and, if necessary, place the hands on the floor beside you for support.

**2** Bend the right leg and place the foot under the left thigh.

**3** Bend the left leg and place the foot under the bent right leg.

**4** Place your hands over respective knees or place one in the other, palms up, on your lap and let them rest.

**5** Keep the body erect without being rigid, and relax the facial muscles.

### NOTE

If the knees are not close to the floor at first, do not be disheartened. As the joints become more flexible and the ligaments more elastic, the knees will come near the floor.

# THE PERFECT POSTURE

**CAUTION**   Avoid this posture if you have varicose veins or venous blood clots. Avoid sitting in this posture if you experience any pain in your pubic area.

**WHAT IT DOES**   As with other folded-legs postures, this sitting position provides a stable base and encourages good posture. It also improves elasticity of the muscles connected to the legs and pelvis.

## HOW TO DO IT

1   Sit comfortably erect with the legs outstretched in front.

2   Bend the left leg and place the sole of the foot against the left thigh as far up as possible.

3   Bend the right leg and slowly and carefully place the foot in the crease formed by the left thigh and calf. Ideally, the right heel should touch the pubic bone.

4   Place the hands over respective knees or rest them, upturned, quietly in the lap.

5   After a while, change the position of the legs so that the right leg is now uppermost.

### NOTE

As in the other cross-legged positions, the knees should ultimately come near to or touch the ground. However, do not force them to do so. Be patient, persevere, and in time they will.

135

# THE FIRM POSTURE (JAPANESE SITTING POSITION)

**CAUTION** Avoid this posture if you have varicose veins or venous blood clots. Avoid sitting in this posture if you experience any pain in your pubic area.

**WHAT IT DOES** A good alternative to sitting on a chair, this posture encourages good spinal alignment and therefore healthier functioning of structures within the trunk.

## HOW TO DO IT

1 Kneel down with the legs together and the body erect but not rigid. Let the feet point straight back.

2 Begin to lower your body very slowly as if to sit on your heels. In so doing, you may find that you will have to incline slightly forward to avoid losing balance. When you have lowered yourself to the point where it is possible to touch the floor beside you, begin to use your hands to assist you in balancing, and also (at the beginning anyway) to share in bearing some of the body's weight. Slowly try to sit upon your heels, but if for the present this is impossible, or your feet cannot bear the weight of your body, then use your hands as suggested.

3 If you have managed to sit on your heels, place the palms of your hands over respective knees, and sit in this manner for a few seconds to begin with; hold the position longer after you are accustomed to the posture. Practise slow, deep, regular breathing.

### SUGGESTION

If you find the weight of your body on your heels too great at first, place a flat cushion or folded towel between buttocks and heels.

complete yoga

# THE SITTING WARRIOR

**CAUTION** Avoid sitting in this posture if you feel the least hint of discomfort in your knees, feet or pubic area. To facilitate sitting in this posture, put one or more cushions under your bottom.

**WHAT IT DOES** The Sitting Warrior is excellent for relieving tired, aching feet and legs. It is also probably the only posture that can safely be used immediately after a heavy meal, as it helps relieve any discomfort that may be felt in the stomach.

## HOW TO DO IT

1 Keeping the body erect but not rigid, kneel down with the knees together but the feet as wide apart as possible, and certainly at least the width of your bottom.

2 Slowly lower your body, using your hands to assist you wherever necessary, and try to sit on the floor between the parted feet. Place your hands over respective knees, or let them lie, one on the other, in your lap.

3 Remain in the pose for as long as you can with absolute comfort, breathing slowly, deeply and evenly.

4 Very slowly and with control come out of the position by reversing the steps for going into the pose. Use your hands to help you. No strain whatever must be placed upon the back.

### DYNAMIC VARIATION

Follow steps 1 and 2. When you can lower yourself no further, let your hands take most of your weight and use them to help you raise yourself up again. Repeat these movements, alternately lowering and raising the body. This improves the blood circulation in the legs.

# THE SQUATTING POSTURE

**CAUTION**    This pose, in its static form, is not recommended for use by persons who have varicose veins. Such persons may, however, practise the dynamic variation. Avoid after the 34th week of pregnancy, until your baby's head is fully engaged, or if you feel any pain in your pubic area. You should not use this posture if you have haemorrhoids, or if you have had a cervical stitch (Shirodkar suture) inserted.

**WHAT IT DOES**    Squatting tones and strengthens the abdominal muscles and helps make the muscles of the pelvic floor more elastic, which is thought to be of value in shortening the period of labour just before the birth. The posture reduces the curve of the spine at the small of the back (this curve may be exaggerated by pregnancy). Consequently, relief is afforded the muscles and ligaments supporting the spine. There is also less pressure on the discs between the bones that make up the spine and, as a result, the back is strengthened and relaxed.

It has been said that the occurrence of breech births is rare among primitive people, and attributed in part to the fact that these people squat a great deal. The incidence of varicose veins, piles, and uterine prolapse appears to be low among people who habitually squat.

## HOW TO DO IT

1   Stand with your legs comfortably apart, taking the body's weight evenly on both feet.

2   Bend the knees slowly, keeping the feet firmly planted on the ground and slowly lower your body until your buttocks come as near as comfortably possible to the heels. When you begin to go down, incline your body somewhat forwards, keeping your arms outstretched, and using them to help you keep your balance. Exhale as you lower yourself. Keep your feet sufficiently wide apart to accommodate your abdomen when you finally manage to sit on your heels. Let your arms hang forwards loosely between your knees, or arrange them in whatever way you find most convenient, perhaps hanging over your knees with your upper arms resting on them.

complete yoga

**3** Hold this position for as long as comfortable, breathing slowly and rhythmically. If you find it easier to place your hands on the floor beside you to help with support and balance, please do so. You must be comfortable.

**4** Inclining slightly forward and using the arms to help with balance, slowly raise the buttocks from the heels and come to a standing position while inhaling. Loosely shake your arms and legs to help them relax.

## DYNAMIC VARIATION

Stand with legs apart and arms at the sides. Inhaling, slowly raise the arms sideways to shoulder level as you simultaneously raise yourself onto your toes. Do not take chances with losing your balance. If necessary, hold on to a stable piece of furniture with one hand as you raise yourself.

Exhale slowly while lowering your arms and body to the squatting position described in step 2 of the Squatting Posture. Without holding the position, come up again on tiptoe, and repeat these up and down movements a few times. Relax.

Alternately lowering and raising the body in this manner contracts and stretches the muscles of the legs. The blood vessels of the legs are gently massaged by the muscular movements, and the flow of blood improved. Pressure on the walls of the blood vessels from a sluggish blood flow is temporarily relieved.

yoga in pregnancy

# THE CAT POSE (PELVIC ROCKING)

These exercises, which are part of the Cat Stretch Sequence (pages 114–115) are best avoided if you have a history of epilepsy.

**WHAT IT DOES** The 'all fours' position also temporarily relieves the pressure the lower back is under when in an upright position. This pressure is caused by the enlarging uterus compressing pelvic blood vessels and impeding blood circulation to the legs and kidneys. In an upright position the uterus also exerts a tremendous pull on the ligaments which attach it to the spine, weakening the lower back. The posture also tones and strengthens the spinal muscles and ligaments, as well as the abdominal muscles, which are then able to support the weight of the enlarging uterus more effectively.

## HOW TO DO IT

**1** Kneel down on 'all fours'. In this position the knees and the palms of the hands are in contact with the floor. The arms and thighs are perpendicular to it, the arms being about shoulder-width apart and the legs comfortably separated. In this position the back is fairly level, like a table on four legs. Since some people's arms and legs are not proportionate, the back may not be absolutely level. Be comfortable.

**2** Exhaling, slowly lower your head, press down on your hands and hunch your shoulders. At the same time tuck your pelvis slightly forwards. These movements should be performed slowly and smoothly to last the length of your exhalation.

**3** Hold the position for a few seconds, breathing normally.

**4** Inhaling, slowly allow your body to relax into the starting position described in step 1. The natural inward curvature of the spine should not be accentuated.

**5** Sit back on your heels or use some other comfortable position in which to relax, breathing normally.

## VARIATION

Get into the 'all fours' position and move your hips from side to side, like an animal wagging its tail. Keep the shoulders facing forward and let the action proceed from the waist.

## SUGGESTIONS

You may use the 'all fours' position when dusting lower parts of furniture, wiping something which has been spilt on the floor, or to amuse a small child. Pause for a few seconds and practise steps 2 to 4.

Performed at bedtime, this posture helps counteract the effects of gravity on your body in its upright position during the day. You will feel more relaxed and probably sleep better after doing it a few times.

## NOTE

The movement that is normally part of the Cat Stretch Sequence that accentuates the concave arch of the lower back is not included in this series of postures as it is not recommended during pregnancy, when it may contribute to backache.

yoga in pregnancy

# THE KNEE PRESS

The Knee Press strengthens the abdominal muscles and the muscles of the neck, shoulders and back. It also relieves back strain and backache. During labour a modification of this pose is usually used when the baby is about to be born. It decreases the space in the abdominal cavity and, together with the breath, exerts pressure on the diaphragm to help push the baby out.

## HOW TO DO IT

**1** Lie on your back, legs outstretched in front and arms alongside the body. Keep the small of the back pressed to the floor as much as possible.

**2** Exhaling, slowly bend the right leg and bring it as close as you can towards the body. If the abdomen is already quite large you will find that you will need to let the knee fall somewhat outwards as you draw it towards you. Now clasp your hands around the bent leg. Keep the shoulders relaxed.

**3** Hold the position for a few seconds, breathing normally.

**4** Inhaling, slowly release the hold on the leg and gradually lower it to the floor. Keep the small of the back pressed to the floor. Relax for a few seconds, breathing normally.

**5** Repeat steps 2 to 4, bending the left leg this time.

## VARIATION 1

1  Follow steps 1 and 2 of the basic exercise.
2  Bend your head forwards and try to touch the bent knee with it.
3  Hold the position for a few seconds, breathing as normally as you can.
4  Release the hold on the leg and carefully lower arms, head, then leg to the floor. Relax, breathing normally.
5  Repeat the exercise with the other leg.

## VARIATION 2

1  Lie as described in step 1 of the basic exercise.
2  Bend one leg, then the other, resting the soles of the feet on the floor. Bring both legs towards the body while exhaling. The legs should be sufficiently separated to accommodate the abdomen without putting pressure on it. Clasp each knee with the corresponding hand, keeping the elbows well out to help maintain the separation of the legs and allow the chest to expand adequately. Now you will be able to breathe deeply. Relax your shoulders.
3  Hold the position for a few seconds, breathing evenly and as deeply as possible.
4  Slowly release the hold on the legs and lower them, one at a time, to the floor. Keep the small of the back pressed to the floor. Relax, breathing normally.

## VARIATION 3

1  Follow steps 1 and 2 of Variation 2.
2  Keeping the legs in this position, bend the head forwards and try to touch the chest with the chin. Keep the shoulders as relaxed as possible.
3  Hold the position for a few seconds, breathing as deeply as comfort permits.
4  Release the hold on each leg in turn and carefully lower it to the floor. Relax, breathing normally.

## NOTES

If you feel more comfortable maintaining the hold on the bent leg or legs by placing your hands underneath rather than over them, please do so.

If you are in the latter part of pregnancy you may find it more comfortable to sit with several pillows behind you in order to practise the postures as described. Arrange your prop so that your back is at about a 45-degree angle to the floor.

yoga in pregnancy

# THE PELVIC TILT

This posture strengthens the lower back and helps relieve fatigue, aches and pain in that area. It also tones and strengthens the abdominal muscles.

## HOW TO DO IT

1 Lie on your back and bend your legs so that the soles of the feet rest comfortably on the floor.

2 Slide your hands under your waist and note the arch in the back. The idea is to remove that arch temporarily. Return your arms to your sides.

3 Establish a comfortable breathing rhythm. Now, on an exhalation, slowly and carefully press the small of your back to the floor to remove the arch. You should feel your abdominal muscles tighten and your pelvis tilt upwards slightly. Hold the position as long as the exhalation lasts.

4 Relax as your inhale.

## SUGGESTIONS

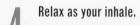

Practise pelvic tilting several times daily by standing against a wall and trying to press the small of the back into it as you exhale. Hold. Relax. When you are in a lift (elevator), try to stand against the side of it and do the same thing.

# THE BRIDGE

**WHAT IT DOES** As with the Pelvic Tilt, this posture strengthens the lower back and helps relieve fatigue, aches and pain in that area. It also tones and strengthens the abdominal muscles.

## HOW TO DO IT

1 Lie on your back with legs outstretched in front and arms alongside the body, palms down.

2 Bend the legs and pull the feet as close to the buttocks as comfortable, keeping the soles firmly on the floor and the legs as close together as you can.

3 Keeping soles, arms and body from the shoulders upwards firmly in contact with the floor, raise the buttocks carefully, slowly, and as high as you can without strain while inhaling. You may find it helpful to press knees, thighs and buttocks firmly together to assist with raising the hips.

4 Hold the position, breathing normally.

5 Slowly reverse the order of the movements while exhaling, and return to the position described in step 1. If you visualize these movements as a slow unrolling of the spine, starting at the shoulder blades, and working toward the bottom, it may help you come out of the posture in the most beneficial way. When you reach the small of the back, press it firmly into the floor.

6 Lying outstretched, or with knees bent and brought close to the body, relax, breathing normally.

yoga in pregnancy

145

# SPINAL TWIST (SIMPLIFIED)

**WHAT IT DOES** The Spinal Twist exercises the usually weak transverse and oblique muscles of the abdomen. It contributes to the flexibility of the spine, and tones the nervous system because of the large number of nerves along the spinal column receiving stimulation. It also aids digestion and helps combat constipation.

## HOW TO DO IT

1 Sit in the Firm Posture (see page 136).

2 Bring the left hand across the front of the body and hold on to the outside of the right thigh. You now have leverage to help with the subsequent twisting action of the trunk. You may place your right hand on the floor beside you for support and balance.

**3** Having established your balance, slowly raise your right hand off the floor to about shoulder level, turning the palm backwards. Inhale as you do this.

**4** Exhaling now, press backwards with the outstretched arm, simultaneously turning your eyes, head and shoulders to follow its movement. The arm movement is reminiscent of a swimming stroke.

**5** When you can turn no farther, bend your elbow and place your hand against your spine, somewhere near the small of your back, with the palm turned away from the body.

**6** Maintain this body twist for a few seconds as you breathe comfortably.

**7** Let the right hand fall and, inhaling, slowly turn your body to face forwards. Rest your hands quietly on your knees and relax, breathing normally.

**8** Repeat steps 2 to 7, twisting to the left this time (substitute 'right' for 'left' in the instructions and vice versa).

## VARIATION

People with varicose veins may welcome an opportunity to practise the Spinal Twist without having to sit on the heels. Sit naturally erect on a chair. Your feet should rest firmly on the floor, toes relaxed, and you should face forwards. Establish a comfortable breathing pattern. Now, on an exhalation, slowly and carefully turn your body from the waist upwards to the left, keeping the pelvis facing forwards and the bottom firmly on the chair. When you can twist no further, hold on to the back of the chair with the left hand, and to your left thigh or side of the chair with your right hand. Look over your left shoulder. Maintain this position for a few seconds, breathing as comfortably as possible. Slowly and carefully come out of the position in reverse order while inhaling, and relax, breathing normally. Repeat the twist to the right side.

yoga in pregnancy

# THE SIDEWAYS SWING

**WHAT IT DOES** The Sideways Swing tones and strengthens the little used transverse and oblique abdominal muscles, and contributes to spinal flexibility.

## HOW TO DO IT

1 Sit upright with both legs bent to the right of the body.

2 Inhaling, raise your arms upwards and interlace your fingers over your head. The upper arms should be alongside your ears.

3 Exhaling, slowly and carefully incline your body sideways in the direction of the legs.

4 Hold the position for two or three seconds, breathing normally.

5 Return to the upright posture, again slowly and carefully, as you inhale. Rest, breathing comfortably.

6 Move the legs to the left side and repeat steps 2 to 5, bending to the left this time. Relax, breathing normally.

complete yoga

Cautions: Please check with your doctor, as you did antenatally, before doing these or any other exercises. The nature of your labour will, to some extent, determine the type of activity suitable for you, and how soon to start it.

Once you have permission to begin exercising, start with gentle all-over stretches such as the Stick Posture (page 52), ankle rotations (page 47) and Diaphragmatic Breathing (page 25). Also practise the Pose of Tranquillity (page 54) every day. Add appropriate exercises to your repertoire as your energy and strength increase.

## Postnatal Sequence

(Practise from 6 weeks postnatally onwards)

| | |
|---|---|
| Warm-ups | Figure of Eight (page 40), Ankle Rotations (page 47), The Butterfly (page 44), Single Leg Raise (page 46), at least 3 times with each leg. |
| Backward- and Forward-bending postures | The Cat Stretch (pages 152–153), paying attention to the cautionary note on page 152 regarding step 2 of the exercise sequence. |
| Sideways-stretching posture | Side Leg Raise (page 104) or the Half Moon (page 105). |
| Twisting posture | Spinal Twist (page 107). |
| Perineal exercise (to strengthen and tone the pelvic floor) | In any comfortable position (lying, sitting, squatting or standing), tighten your perineum (lowest part of your torso, between the external genitals and the anus) on an exhalation. Hold the tightness as long as your exhalation lasts. Release the tightness as you breathe regularly. Repeat the exercise periodically during the day. |
| Relaxation | The Crocodile (page 150). |
| Breathing exercise | Anti-Anxiety Breath (page 28). |
| Meditative exercise | Candle Concentration (page 121). |

yoga in pregnancy

# THE CROCODILE

**CAUTION**   Lying prone without some support under the hips is not recommended. It would accentuate the curve of the spine at the lower back, and place strain on the muscles and ligaments in that area.

**WHAT IT DOES**   The Crocodile helps flatten the abdomen more quickly and assists the uterus in returning to its normal position. The posture also contributes to complete physical and mental relaxation.

## HOW TO DO IT

1 Lie prone (face down), body stretched out at full length, limbs relaxed. The toes should point toward each other and the heels fall apart. Arms should lie passively on either side of the body or folded above the head; the face is turned to one side. Change the direction to which your face is turned after a while or the next time you lie in this position.

2 Either place a pillow under your head or make a 'pillow' of your arms and rest your head on this.

3 Place one or two pillows under the hips and abdomen. This will reduce the arch at the small of the back and prevent strain on the back muscles.

4 Your breasts should fall freely between the two sets of pillows and not be compressed. Compression may cause pain, especially if you are nursing.

5 Follow the same relaxation technique as in the Pose of Tranquillity (see page 54).

### NOTE

Use this position, especially during the first few days post partum, when having your afternoon nap.

# LEG OVER

**WHAT IT DOES** This posture firms and strengthens the oblique and transverse abdominal muscles and those of the lower back. It trims the waistline, and tones and helps slenderize the inner thighs.

## HOW TO DO IT

1 Lie on your back with legs together and outstretched. Position your arms so they are pointing sideways, at shoulder level. Your body and limbs should resemble a letter 'T'. Keep your back pressed firmly to the surface on which you are lying.

2 Raise the left leg slowly upwards and then across the body to touch the floor on your right side. Do this either on exhalation or inhalation. Simultaneously turn the head to the left, keeping the hands, arms and shoulders in contact with the floor.

3 Hold for a second or two, breathing normally. Combining suitable breathing, slowly bring the left leg up and lower it to the floor in front of you.

4 Relax, breathing normally. Repeat steps 2 and 3, this time raising the right leg and turning the head to the right. (Substitute 'right' for 'left' and vice versa, in the instructions.)

### NOTE

The Leg Over is more effective if the hands, arms and shoulders are kept in contact with the floor, even if you cannot lower the leg as much as you would wish.

yoga in pregnancy

151

# THE CAT STRETCH

**CAUTION**     It is very important to check with your doctor before practising the following exercise sequence. Step 2, done earlier than six weeks following the birth of your baby, poses risks of air emboli (air bubbles in the blood vessels or chambers of the heart).

**WHAT IT DOES**     The Cat Stretch tones and strengthens the muscles of the back and abdomen, helps keep the spine supple and helps relieve backache. The posture also assists the uterus in returning to its normal position, and improves the pelvic blood circulation. (During pregnancy the weight of the uterus compresses pelvic blood vessels, slowing down the circulation.)

## HOW TO DO IT

**1** With arms and legs comfortably apart, adopt an 'all fours' position on hands and knees. Thighs and arms should be roughly perpendicular to the trunk.

**2** Inhaling, bend your elbows and attempt to lower the chest to the floor. Thighs should remain perpendicular to the body, and the back should not be allowed to sag. Keep the head bent slightly backward so that the neck receives a delightful stretch as the chin also touches the floor. Let the hands and arms take most of the weight so that no undesirable pressure is exerted on the lower back.

**3** Hold the position for several seconds, breathing normally.

complete yoga

152

**4** Exhaling, return to the starting position described in step 1. Remain thus for a few seconds, breathing normally.

**5** Exhaling, lower your head and hunch your back. Bring your left knee towards your forehead. Hold the position for a second or two.

**6** Inhaling, push the leg backwards and stretch it up as far as you can, while bringing the head up and back. Keep the leg as straight as possible. Hold for a second or two, breathing normally.

**7** Exhaling, lower the knee to the floor and relax for a few seconds, breathing normally. Relax the neck.

**8** Repeat steps 5 to 7, using the right leg this time.

**9** Lie down and relax, breathing slowly and rhythmically.

## NOTES

Step 2 describes what is known in medical circles as the 'knee-chest' position. When this position is held, the pressure of abdominal viscera on pelvic organs is relieved, and the uterus gravitates forward into its normal position.

The posture is therefore useful in helping correct retroversion (tipping backward) of the uterus. It is a fairly common condition following repeated childbearing, and may be due to excessive relaxation of some pelvic structures. Signs and symptoms of this condition include backache and persistent vaginal discharge.

In addition to being used as part of the Cat Stretch series, this pose may be used as a complete asana in itself. Practised daily, it will help the uterus return to its prepregnant position speedily. Please refer to the caution on page 152 preceding the instructions for this exercise sequence. Adjust the position of the arms and hands for maximum comfort (try turning the hands so that the fingers point toward each other). Remember not to exert too much downward pressure on the small of the back, and make sure that the bladder is empty before you begin practice.

chapter eight

# yoga for good health

As previously mentioned, yoga means integration or wholeness. And vital to that wholeness is our health. This chapter offers guidance on healthy eating, as well as an in-depth guide to the role of nutrients, their food sources and the effects of any deficiency. This is followed by a number of hygienic practices that are particularly useful incorporated into your daily routine. The final section is dedicated to an A–Z of ailments. This offers guidance on utilizing nutrients and yoga practices to assist in the prevention and treatment of health disorders.

# EATING HEALTHILY AND FOODS TO AVOID

◆ Reduce your intake of high-fat foods, which contribute to heart and blood vessel diseases.

◆ Avoid high-protein diets, which place extra demands on the body and can increase the need for other nutrients.

◆ Ensure a regular intake of dietary fibre to help prevent disorders such as constipation, piles and varicose veins.

◆ Eat plenty of complex carbohydrates ('slowly-digested carbohydrates') such as whole grain breads and pasta, potatoes, and fresh fruit and vegetables, to provide important nutrients and bulk, to regulate bowel function and contribute to a trim, healthy body.

◆ Avoid using over-processed foods (including many convenience foods) which are often devoid of many essential nutrients.

◆ Reduce sodium (salt) added to food during preparation and cooking, and also at the table. High sodium intake has been linked to high blood pressure.

◆ Cut down consumption of refined sugars, which have been implicated in conditions such as tooth decay, obesity, diabetes and high cholesterol levels.

◆ Decrease or eliminate your caffeine intake. Instead, drink beverages such as water, unsweetened fruit juices, freshly pressed vegetable juices, herbal teas and milk.

◆ Consume less or avoid any substances known to be antagonistic to essential nutrients, such as alcohol, cigarette smoke and commercial laxatives.

◆ If you are troubled by symptoms of low blood sugar (hypoglycaemia), replace your regular three large meals with five or six small wholesome meals evenly spaced throughout the day, to help maintain adequate blood sugar levels.

◆ Store, prepare and cook food in ways that conserve nutrients. Try to make mealtimes pleasant and unhurried, and do not overeat.

# HEALING NUTRIENTS

Nutrition aims at promoting and maintaining good health, and rebuilding it when it has broken down. It is often a slow process; seldom as quick and dramatic, for example, as preventing the spread of infection with antibiotics. Studies indicate, however, that repairing the body through nutrition can be much more rapid than was formerly believed.

It is essentially what we eat that supplies the raw material for building and repairing the body's various components. Nutrients from the diet are processed by the digestive system and transported to every cell, tissue and organ through the circulatory system.

When there is a wound or infection, the body's demand for certain nutrients increases. As healing occurs, the body uses up nutrients at a greater rate than usual, as it does under other forms of stress. But it is as well to bear in mind that all nutrients work together for the harmonious functioning of the entire system.

If you are considering taking nutritional supplements, please first consult a nutritionist, a dietician or other qualified health professional. Some vitamins and minerals taken indiscriminately can be toxic.

# VITAMINS

## VITAMIN A (RETINOL)

Vitamin A is essential for maintaining healthy hair, skin and the mucous membranes that line body cavities and tubular organs. It is helpful in treating acne. Formerly known as the 'anti-infection' vitamin, vitamin A builds resistance to infections such as respiratory diseases. It is necessary for counteracting night blindness and weak eyesight, and helps in the treatment of several eye disorders. Useful in the treatment of an overactive thyroid gland, it also promotes the growth of strong bones, and protects the lining of joints against inflammation. Like vitamins C and E, vitamin A is an antioxidant: it averts certain types of oxygen damage. Vitamin A deficiency may result in skin, hair and nail problems, and in problems of the digestive, urinary and respiratory systems. It leads to an increased susceptibility to infections and certain eye problems (including night blindness), as well as fatigue and low energy.

Good vitamin A sources include fresh vegetables, especially the intensely green and yellow ones such as asparagus, broccoli, carrots, dandelion leaves, kale, parsley, spinach, squash, sweet potatoes and turnip tops; fresh fruits, especially apricots, cantaloupe melons, cherries, mangoes, papaya and peaches; milk and milk products; and fish liver oils.

## CAROTENOIDS (CAROTENES)

Carotenes represent the most widespread group of naturally occurring pigments in plant life. Many people equate the term 'carotene' with pro-vitamin A, but only 30–50 of the more than 400 carotenoids are believed to have vitamin A activity. Recent evidence indicates that carotenes have many more activities than serving simply as a vitamin A precursor. Although research has focused primarily on betacarotene, other carotenes are more potent in their antioxidant activity, and are deposited in tissues to a greater degree.

Foods rich in betacarotene are also rich in the many other carotenoids. A high intake of these substances is associated with a reduced rate of cancers involving epithelial cells (lungs, skin, cervix, respiratory tract, gastrointestinal tract, and so on).

The consumption of foods rich in carotenes (such as green leafy vegetables, yams, sweet potatoes, carrots, broccoli, squash, cantaloupe melons and apricots) offers significant benefits to the immune system.

## THE B VITAMINS

Called 'the nerve vitamins', this complex consists of more than 20 vitamins, essential for maintaining a healthy nervous system and for helping counteract the harmful effects of stress. In addition, they help build and repair the body's cells to produce healthy skin, hair and nails. The B vitamins affect all components of the immune system, which protects us from threats of infection and other forms of disease. Deficiency of any of the B vitamins can result in low energy levels. The harder you work and the less sleep you get, the greater is your need for these vitamins.

The B-complex vitamins are present in brewer's yeast, green leafy vegetables, legumes (dried peas, beans and lentils), wheat germ and whole grains and cereals.

The individual vitamins within the B complex are as follows:

## B1 (Thiamine)

Thiamine is important for growth. It aids appetite and is necessary for proper digestion, especially of carbohydrates. It is essential for normal functioning of nervous tissue, and keeps muscles (including the heart muscle) functioning normally. It helps combat travel sickness, and it has been found useful in relieving post-operative pain. Thiamine deficiency results in a loss of appetite, impaired digestion, irritable bowel syndrome, constipation and diarrhoea. It can cause various types of nervous disorder and a loss of the coordination power of muscles, as well as fatigue and weakness. Thiamine deficiency may also produce beriberi, early symptoms of which include fatigue, irritability, poor memory, sleep disturbance, loss of appetite, constipation and abdominal discomfort.

Good thiamine sources include Brazil nuts, brewer's yeast, buckwheat flour, cantaloupe melons, green leafy vegetables, legumes, potatoes, rolled oats, soya beans, sunflower seeds, whole grains and yellow cornmeal.

## B2 (Riboflavin)

Riboflavin is important for the formation of certain enzymes. It aids growth and reproduction, and promotes healthy skin, hair and nails. It helps prevent or heal a sore mouth, tongue and lips. It eases eye fatigue and benefits vision. Riboflavin deficiency may result in weakness, anaemia, impaired growth, skin problems, intolerance of light (photophobia), inflamed tongue, cracks at the corners of the mouth (cheilosis) and a lowered resistance to infection.

Good riboflavin sources include almonds, brewer's yeast, broccoli, buckwheat flour, cantaloupe melons, dark green leafy vegetables, legumes, lima (butter) beans, milk and milk products, mushrooms, sunflower seeds, wheat germ, whole grains and wild rice.

## B3 (Niacin, Nicotinic Acid, Nicotinamide)

Vitamin B3 is considered an antioxidant, much like vitamins A, C and E. It helps to promote a healthy digestive system and to alleviate disturbances of the stomach and intestines. Other vitamin B3 roles include promoting healthy skin, helping prevent and ease the severity of migraine headaches, improving blood circulation, reducing cholesterol and high blood pressure, helping counteract the unpleasant symptoms of vertigo, assisting the healing of canker sores, and sometimes combating bad breath. It also increases energy as it promotes the body's proper utilization of food. Vitamin B3 deficiency can result in weakness, digestive disorders, irritability and depression.

Good vitamin B3 sources include artichokes, asparagus, brewer's yeast, green leafy vegetables, legumes, nuts, potatoes, seeds, whole grains and whole-grain products.

## B5 (Pantothenic Acid, Pantothenol, Calcium Pantothenate)

Vitamin B5 enhances immunity to disease. It helps wounds to heal and is useful in preventing fatigue and increasing energy. It counteracts skin inflammations and is important for the normal functioning of adrenal gland secretions, which play a vital role in stress reactions. A vitamin B5 deficiency may produce low blood sugar (hypoglycaemia), duodenal ulcers, fatigue and blood and skin disorders. When vitamin B5 is deficient in the diet, fats burn at only half their normal rate – a fact worth remembering when you are trying to lose weight and increase energy.

Vitamin B5 may be obtained from avocados, brewer's yeast, broccoli, brown rice, cabbage, cauliflower, hazelnuts, green vegetables, legumes, milk, mushrooms, pecan nuts, potatoes, sunflower seeds, sweet potatoes, tomatoes, unrefined vegetable oils, wheat germ and whole grains.

### B6 (Pyridoxine)

Pyridoxine is important for maintaining a good resistance to disease. It is needed for the proper assimilation of protein and fat, and for the production of hormones. It aids in the conversion of tryptophan (an essential amino acid) to niacin, helps prevent various nervous and skin disorders, and alleviates nausea. It also promotes the synthesis of anti-ageing nucleic acids, and is helpful in reducing leg cramps, nocturnal muscle spasms, hand numbness and certain nerve inflammations of the extremities. An additional role for vitamin B6 is as a natural diuretic. A pyridoxine deficiency can result in anaemia, dandruff, skin problems, inflamed nerves, loss of appetite, nausea, vomiting and an inflamed tongue.

Good pyridoxine sources include apples, asparagus, avocados, bananas, blackstrap molasses, brewer's yeast, brown rice, buckwheat flour, cabbage, cantaloupe melons, carrots, eggs, hazelnuts, green leafy vegetables, milk, peas, prunes, raisins, sunflower seeds, tomatoes, wheat germ, whole grains and whole-grain products.

### B9 (Folate, Folacin, Folic Acid)

Vitamin B9 is essential for the normal functioning of the system responsible for the production and development of blood cells. It plays an important role in keeping the immune system working effectively, and can be useful as a pain reliever. Used in conjunction with vitamin B5 and PABA (para-aminobenzoic acid), it may delay the greying of hair. A vitamin B9 deficiency can cause anaemia, two symptoms of which are fatigue and shortness of breath. It can also affect the proper formation of the body's disease-fighting cells, and be a contributing factor in excessive hair loss.

Good vitamin B9 sources include apricots, avocados, beans, carrots, egg yolk, green leafy vegetables, spring onions, pumpkin, tempeh, torula yeast, wheat germ and whole-grain products.

### B12 (Cobalamin, Cyano-cobalamin)

Vitamin B12 is essential for the production and regeneration of red blood cells. It helps maintain a healthy nervous system and is useful for improving memory, concentration and balance. It is important for the body's proper utilization of fats, carbohydrates and protein, and may also have a regulating effect on the immune system. Women may find this nutrient helpful just before and during menstruation. Vitamin B12 deficiency may result in anaemia or in brain damage.

Good food sources include eggs, milk products and tempeh.

### B15 (Pangamic Acid)

Vitamin B15 extends the life span of cells. It helps to lower blood cholesterol levels and relieve the symptoms of angina pectoris and asthma. It protects against pollutants, helps to prevent cirrhosis of the liver, neutralizes the craving for alcohol and helps to fend off hangovers. Vitamin B15 speeds recovery from fatigue, stimulates immunity responses and assists in protein synthesis. Vitamin B15 deficiency may be linked to glandular and nervous disorders, heart disease and diminished oxygenation of tissues.

This vitamin may be obtained from brewer's yeast, brown rice, pumpkin seeds, sesame seeds and whole grains.

### Biotin (coenzyme R, Vitamin H)

Biotin is associated with the vitamin B complex and is necessary for the body's effective utilization of this group of vitamins. Important for carbohydrate metabolism, it is needed for a healthy nervous system, and can help prevent hair from turning grey and from falling out excessively. It is also useful for alleviating skin inflammations and muscle pains. A biotin deficiency could result in eczema of the face and body, loss of appetite, insomnia, irritability, depression and extreme exhaustion.

Good biotin sources include brewer's yeast, brown rice, egg yolk, fresh fruits, legumes, nuts, wheat germ and whole grains.

### Choline

Choline is another member of the vitamin B complex. It helps control the build-up of cholesterol and aids in the transmission of nerve impulses, especially those involved with memory. It helps to eliminate poisons and drugs from the system through the liver. A choline deficiency may lead to liver disorders, a hardening of the arteries and possibly Alzheimer's disease.

Good choline sources include egg yolk, green leafy vegetables, lecithin and wheat germ.

### Inositol

Inositol is yet another member of the vitamin B complex. It can help lower cholesterol levels, promote healthy hair and prevent excessive hair loss. It may help counteract eczema and be useful in the redistribution of body fat. It also aids in preventing constipation. Inositol deficiency may result in eczema and contribute to abnormal hair loss (alopecia).

The best natural sources of inositol include brewer's yeast, cabbage, cantaloupe melons, grapefruit, dried lima (butter) beans, molasses (unrefined), peanuts, raisins and wheat germ.

## PABA (Para-aminobenzoic Acid)

This member of the vitamin B complex is important for healthy intestines, effective metabolism, and the proper formation of blood cells. It can help to keep skin healthy and to delay wrinkles, and has been known to aid in restoring natural colour to the hair. Used as an ointment, it is helpful for protection against sunburn. PABA deficiency symptoms include fatigue, digestive disorders, headaches, nervousness, depression and constipation. PABA deficiency can also result in eczema and the greying of hair.

Like other B-complex vitamins, PABA is supplied by brewer's yeast, eggs, green leafy vegetables, molasses, rice bran (rice polish), wheat germ, whole grains and yoghurt.

## Anti-stress Factors

Associated with the B complex, these are vitamin-like substances which have a protective action against the impact of various stressors. In clinical tests, laboratory rats subjected to chemical stressors (for example, aspirin and cortisone) suffered adverse reactions that could not be reversed through supplementation with certain nutrients. When given foods containing the anti-stress factors, however, they were found to be fully protected. Research suggests that those suffering from ill health benefit from incorporating into their diet as many foods as possible that contain these nutrients.

The anti-stress factors are found in green leafy vegetables, some nutritional yeasts, soya flour (from which the oil has not been removed) and wheat germ.

## VITAMIN C (ASCORBIC ACID)

This vitamin is essential for the formation and maintenance of collagen — a cement-like substance that holds together the cells forming a variety of tissues including skin, cartilage and bone. Vitamin C, an anti-stress vitamin, is needed to build resistance to disease and for various healing processes. It also contributes to the body's utilization of oxygen and to its maintenance of a healthy blood circulation. Like vitamins A and E, it is an antioxidant, helping to slow down the destructive effects of oxygen and other substances. Other vitamin C roles include helping to decrease blood cholesterol levels, reducing the incidence of blood clots in veins, aiding in the prevention and easing of symptoms of the common cold, reducing the effects of many allergy-producing substances, and acting as a natural laxative. It also facilitates the absorption of iron. Vitamin C deficiency may result in a lowered resistance to infections, tender joints and a susceptibility to gum and tooth disease. If the deficiency is severe, anaemia or haemorrhage can occur, as can scurvy.

The best vitamin C sources include fresh fruits such as apricots, blackberries, blueberries, cantaloupe melons, cherries, elderberries, gooseberries, grapefruit, guavas, honeydew melons, kiwi fruit, kumquats, lemons, limes, oranges, papaya, rosehips and strawberries; and fresh vegetables such as cabbage, dandelion leaves, green and red peppers, kohlrabi, mustard and cress and turnip tops.

## Flavonoids

Associated with vitamin C, these compounds – responsible for the colours of fruits and flowers – offer remarkable protection against free radical damage. (Free radicals are molecules produced by oxidation during normal metabolic processes. They can damage the membranes and genetic material of cells, and have been implicated in cancerous tissue changes, heart and lung disease, cataracts and premature ageing.) While flavonoids protect plants against environmental stress, in humans they appear to function as biological response modifiers as indicated by their anti-inflammatory, anti-allergic, anti-viral and anti-carcinogenic activity.

Flavonoids increase the effectiveness of vitamin C, strengthen the walls of capillaries and veins, help build resistance to infection, prevent gums from bleeding and promote their healing, and are useful in the treatment of oedema (swelling) and dizziness from disease of the inner ear.

The best way to ensure an adequate intake of flavonoids is to eat a varied diet, rich in fresh fruits and vegetables.

## VITAMIN D (CALCIFEROL)

Vitamin D regulates the absorption of calcium and phosphorus from the intestines and assists in the assimilation of vitamin A. Taken with vitamins A and C, it can help prevent colds. It is also useful in treating conjunctivitis, an inflammation of the mucous membrane that lines the eyelids. Mild vitamin-D deficiency interferes with the body's utilization of calcium in bone and teeth formation. In children, a severe deficiency may lead to rickets (which results in abnormal bone development); and in adults to osteomalacia, (in which bones soften) and senile osteoporosis (in which there is increased bone porosity in later life).

Vitamin D may be obtained through the action of sunlight on the skin; from vitamin D-enriched milk; and from butter, eggs, fish and fish liver oils.

## VITAMIN E (TOCOPHEROL)

Vitamin E, one of the anti-stress vitamins, is an active antioxidant; it prevents oxidation of vitamin A, selenium, some vitamin C and fat compounds. It also enhances vitamin A activity. Vitamin E plays an important role as a vasodilator (an agent that widens blood vessels) and thus improves circulation. As an anti-coagulant, it dissolves and helps prevent blood clots. It also works as a diuretic, increasing the flow of urine, and it can lower high blood pressure. Vitamin E can help keep you looking younger by slowing down cellular ageing resulting from oxidation. It helps supply oxygen to the body, improving levels of endurance and alleviating fatigue. Along with vitamin C, it can protect the lungs against air pollution. Vitamin E may prevent ugly scar formation if taken internally and applied to the area involved by piercing the ends of a vitamin E capsule and squeezing the oil onto it. It can also accelerate the healing of burns, aid in preventing miscarriages, and help ease unpleasant menopausal symptoms. Vitamin E deficiency may result in the destruction of red blood cells and some forms of anaemia. It may be a factor in certain reproductive disorders, and in kidney and liver damage.

Good vitamin E sources include almonds and other nuts, broccoli, Brussels sprouts, eggs, fresh fruits, green leafy vegetables, legumes, seeds, unrefined vegetable oils, wheat germ and whole grains.

## EFAS (ESSENTIAL FATTY ACIDS, POLYUNSATURATED FATTY ACIDS)

Two classes of fatty acids are considered essential (essential, in this case, means that our body needs them but cannot produce them, so we require them from foods). These are the omega-3 and omega-6 fatty acids. EFAs are a vital part of the structure of every cell in the body. They are also a necessary component of the fatty film that coats the skin's surface, a film that is important for protection against the entry of disease-causing organisms. EFAs play a role in cholesterol metabolism and in blood clotting. They help provide energy, maintain body temperature, insulate nerves, cushion and protect tissues, and promote healthy skin, hair and nails. EFAs, moreover, aid in weight reduction by burning saturated fats. EFA deficiency may result in acne and eczema. Other deficiency symptoms include poor reproductive capacity, heart and blood-circulation disorders, faulty healing of wounds, dried-up tear ducts and salivary glands, lowered resistance to infection, improper formation of collagen and abnormal hair loss.

Generally the best source of EFAs are the oils of certain seeds and nuts, such as flax seed, sunflower, sesame and evening primrose. Other good sources include wheat germ, soya bean and peanut oils, almonds, avocados, peanuts, pecans, sunflower seeds and walnuts. (Although most nuts provide some EFAs, Brazil and cashew nuts do not.)

## VITAMIN K (MENADIONE, MENAPHTHONE)

Also known as 'the blood vitamin', vitamin K promotes proper blood clotting and helps to prevent bleeding. It is also now considered important in helping to prevent osteoporosis. Vitamin K also aids in reducing excessive menstrual flow. A vitamin K deficiency could result in colitis (inflammation of the large intestine) and sprue (symptoms of which include weakness, weight loss and various digestive disorders).

A varied, wholesome diet generally provides an adequate supply of vitamin K for normal requirements. Rich food sources, however, include alfalfa sprouts, cow's milk, egg yolk, fish liver oils, green leafy vegetables and kelp; also safflower, soya bean and other unrefined vegetable oils.

# MINERALS

## BORON

The trace mineral boron has been shown to safeguard calcium in the body. It appears to be necessary for activating vitamin D, as well as certain hormones, including oestrogen. Boron, moreover, elevates the concentration of the most biologically active form of oestrogen in the blood – oestrogen administration has proved to be effective for slowing calcium loss from bone in postmenopausal women.

Fresh fruits and vegetables are the main sources of boron. These include alfalfa sprouts, cabbage, lettuce, peas, sugar snap beans, apples and grapes; also soya beans, dates, prunes and raisins. Boron may also be obtained from almonds, hazelnuts and peanuts.

### Caution

Since the human requirement for boron has not yet been established, and the results of long-term toxicity studies have yet to be reported, boron supplementation is not recommended. You can increase boron intake, however, by including boron-rich foods in your diet.

## CALCIUM

Considered an anti-stress mineral, calcium is needed for the proper functioning of nervous tissue, for good muscle tone, normal blood clotting and for the maintenance of sound bones and healthy teeth. Calcium is required to keep your heart beating regularly. It helps metabolize your body's iron and can aid in combating insomnia. It is also needed to maintain a sound chemical balance in the body. In order for calcium to be absorbed, vitamin D supplies must be adequate. Vitamin C and lactose (milk sugar) enhance calcium absorption. Emotional stress and prolonged bed rest increase calcium requirements; as do high-fat and high-protein diets. Calcium deficiency results in the wasting of energy, an inability to relax and can also lead to rickets, osteomalacia and osteoporosis.

The best food sources of calcium include blackstrap molasses, carob flour (powder), citrus fruits, dried beans, dried figs, green vegetables, milk and milk products, peanuts, sesame seeds, soya beans, sunflower seeds and walnuts.

### CHLORINE

This mineral aids digestion and is essential for the formation of hydrochloric acid in the stomach. It helps keep you flexible since it aids in stimulating and regulating muscular action. A chlorine deficiency may contribute to the loss of hair and teeth.

The best natural sources of chlorine include kelp and olives.

### CHROMIUM

Useful in helping to prevent and to lower high blood pressure, chromium also works as a preventive against diabetes. Chromium deficiency is suspected to be a factor in arteriosclerosis (the hardening of arteries) and diabetes.

The best natural chromium sources include brewer's yeast and corn oil. Refined foods are often stripped of chromium.

### COBALT

Cobalt is part of vitamin B12 and is, therefore, essential for red blood cells. It also helps in preventing anaemia. A cobalt deficiency can result in anaemia and its associated loss of energy.

Good natural cobalt sources include green leafy vegetables, kelp, torula yeast and whole grains grown on mineral-rich soils.

### COPPER

Copper is an essential trace mineral which plays an important role in many enzyme systems. It helps in the development and functioning of nerve, brain and connective tissue. It is needed in small amounts to help synthesize haemoglobin – the colouring matter of red blood cells, which is often low in anaemia. It is also required to convert the body's iron into haemoglobin and is essential for the utilization of vitamin C. Copper deficiency decreases the absorption of iron and shortens the life span of red blood cells. These deficiencies contribute to anaemia. A copper deficiency may also lead to oedema (swelling).

If you eat an adequate supply of green leafy vegetables and whole-grain products, it is unlikely that you will have to worry about copper deficiency. Other food sources of this nutrient are legumes, nuts and prunes.

## FLUORINE (FLUORIDE)

This mineral is vital to general well-being. It works with calcium to strengthen bones and is also important for sound teeth. Fluoride deficiency may lead to tooth decay.

Organic fluorine is found in almonds, beetroot tops, carrots, garlic, green vegetables, milk and cheese, steel-cut oats and sunflower seeds. It is normally present in seawater and in naturally hard water.

## IODINE (IODIDE)

Iodine can help with weight control by burning excess fat. It contributes to the maintenance of good energy levels, helps maintain mental alertness, and promotes healthy hair, skin, nails and teeth. Two-thirds of the body's iodine is in the thyroid gland. Since this gland controls metabolism, an insufficient supply of iodine can result in slow mental reaction, lack of energy and weight gain. Iodine deficiency can also lead to goitre – an enlargement of the thyroid gland, which is still not uncommon in areas where the soil is iodine deficient. (Symptoms of goitre include rapid heartbeat, nervous irritability and anaemia.)

The best natural sources of iodine include broccoli, cabbage, carrots, garlic, lettuce, onion, pineapple and foods grown in iodine-rich, coastal soils.

## IRON

Iron is required for the proper metabolism of the B vitamins and, together with the minerals cobalt, copper and manganese, is necessary for the assimilation of vitamin C. Iron is a vital component of haemoglobin, which transports oxygen to all body cells. It is, moreover, an essential part of immune system enzymes and proteins, and important for the vitality of germ-killing cells. Vitamin C facilitates the absorption of iron. An iron deficiency leads to anaemia.

Perhaps the greatest single cause of iron deficiency is the refining of breads, cereals and sugar. Although iron is added to so-called enriched flour, this food item is not a rich source compared, for example, with brewer's yeast and wheat germ. Other commendable food sources of iron include artichokes, asparagus, blackstrap molasses, Brussels sprouts, cauliflower, dried fruits, egg yolk, kiwi fruit, leafy vegetables, seaweed, seeds, sharon fruit (persimmon), strawberries, watermelon and whole grains.

### Caution

Unless you are a menstruating woman or have suffered a significant loss of blood, you should not take iron supplements except as prescribed by your doctor. Excess iron can accumulate in the body to toxic levels, which can interfere with immunity and possibly promote cancer. If you take a multivitamin and/or multimineral supplement, make sure it does not contain iron – unless iron has been prescribed for you.

## MAGNESIUM

Magnesium is needed by every cell in the body since it is essential for the body's synthesis of protein and for the utilization of fats, the B vitamins and several minerals. It acts as an important catalyst in many enzyme reactions: most of these enzymes contain vitamin B6, which is not well absorbed unless magnesium is adequately provided by the diet. Known as an anti-stress mineral, magnesium aids in combating depression and in promoting a healthy cardiovascular system (heart and blood vessels). It helps to keep teeth healthy and to prevent the formation of stones in the kidneys and gall bladder. It can also relieve indigestion. Alcoholics are usually deficient in magnesium. The symptoms of magnesium deficiency include fatigue, weakness, nervous tension and insomnia. These are often remedied when magnesium is supplied. In fact, magnesium may be regarded as one of nature's tranquillizers.

The milling of grains – with the consequent removal of the bran and germ – has substantially affected magnesium intake. White flour, for instance, has only 22 per cent of the magnesium present in whole-wheat flour. The best magnesium sources include alfalfa sprouts, almonds and other nuts eaten fresh from the shell, apples, beetroot tops, blackstrap molasses, brown rice, celery, chard, dried fruits (including figs), grapefruits, green leafy vegetables grown on mineral-rich soils, oranges, peas, potatoes, sesame seeds, soya beans, sunflower seeds, wheat bran, wheat germ and whole grains.

## MANGANESE

Manganese helps activate enzymes necessary for the body's proper use of biotin, vitamin B1 and vitamin C. It is needed for sound bone structure and for the formation of thyroxin, the principal hormone of the thyroid gland. Manganese is also required for the proper digestion and utilization of food, and is important for the normal functioning of the nervous and reproductive systems. Because of its role in these vital body functions, manganese can help reduce fatigue and irritability, and improve memory.

The best natural manganese sources include beetroot, egg yolk, green leafy vegetables, nuts, peas and whole-grain cereals.

## MOLYBDENUM

This mineral forms a vital part of the enzyme responsible for the body's iron utilization. It can help prevent anaemia and promote general well-being. Molybdenum deficiency may contribute to dental caries, male impotence, irritability and an irregular heartbeat.

The best food sources of this nutrient include dark-green leafy vegetables, legumes and whole grains.

## PHOSPHORUS

Phosphorus works with calcium to build bones and teeth. It helps maintain normal brain and nerve tissue. A phosphorus deficiency results in weight loss, loss of appetite, irregular breathing and fatigue.

Food sources of phosphorus include corn, dairy products (low-fat), dried fruits, egg yolks, legumes, nuts, seeds and whole grains.

## POTASSIUM

Together with the mineral sodium, potassium helps maintain the electrical and chemical balance between tissue cells and the blood. These two nutrients must be in balance in order to maintain muscle contractions and the normal transmission of nerve signals. Potassium plays an important part in the release of energy from carbohydrates, proteins and fats. When the sodium level is high in proportion to that of potassium, health problems such as muscle weakness, mental confusion and heart disorders may occur. Potassium can contribute to clear thinking by facilitating the supply of oxygen to the brain. It can help dispose of body wastes, reduce high blood pressure and enhance allergy treatment.

Low blood sugar (hypoglycaemia) causes potassium loss, as does severe diarrhoea or a long fast. Both mental and physical stress can lead to potassium deficiency, which may result in oedema (swelling) and in hypoglycaemia.

Foods in their natural state offer the best sources of potassium, without being too high in sodium. These include bananas, cereals (whole grain), citrus fruit, green leafy vegetables, legumes, mint leaves, nuts, potatoes, watercress and watermelon.

## SELENIUM

Selenium is a trace mineral needed to maintain healthy circulation and to reinforce the body's immune system. It works with vitamins C and E to help detoxify the body and keep it free of harmful substances (selenium is an antioxidant). It may play a part in neutralizing certain cancer-producing agents. Men appear to have a greater need for selenium than women. Almost half of their body's supply concentrates in the testicles and parts of the seminal ducts near the prostate gland. Selenium is lost in semen. Selenium helps preserve the youthful elasticity of tissues. It can ease hot flushes and other discomforts of menopause. It is also useful in preventing and treating dandruff. Selenium deficiency may result in loss of stamina.

The best food sources of this nutrient include cider vinegar, asparagus, brewer's yeast, eggs, garlic, mushrooms, sesame seeds, unrefined cereals, wheat germ, whole grains and whole-grain products.

## SILICON (SILICA)

Some skin experts say that this trace mineral gives life to the skin and lustre to the hair. Silicon is essential for both the hardness and flexibility of bones. It hastens the healing of fractures, reduces scarring at fracture sites, and contributes to the building up of connective tissue. It is also required for the normal functioning of the adrenal glands which are involved in stress reactions.

Foods made from natural buckwheat are a rich source of this micro-nutrient. Other sources include apples, asparagus, barley, beetroot, brown rice, carrots, celery, cherries, corn, eggs, green leafy vegetables, green and red peppers, lentils, lettuce, millet, mushrooms, oats, onions, pears, potatoes, parsley, pumpkin, rye, strawberries, tomatoes and whole wheat.

## SODIUM

Sodium is necessary to preserve a balance between calcium and potassium in order to maintain normal heart action and the equilibrium of the body. It regulates body fluids (sodium, potassium and chlorine play an important role in keeping body fluids near a neutral pH). Sodium-deficiency symptoms include weakness, nerve disorders, weight loss and disturbed digestion.

Natural sodium sources include asparagus, beetroot, carrots, celery, courgettes (zucchini), egg yolks (raw), figs, marrow (squash), oatmeal, string beans and turnips.

## SULPHUR

Sulphur is essential for the formation of body tissues and is also needed for tissue respiration. It is part of the vitamin B complex and is required for collagen synthesis. Known as 'the beauty mineral', sulphur helps keep the hair glossy and the complexion clear.

Food sources of sulphur include beans, bran, Brussels sprouts, cabbage, egg yolks, garlic, horseradish, kale, onions, peppers (all kinds) and radishes.

## VANADIUM

This trace mineral may be related to the regulation of electrolytes (such as sodium, potassium and chlorine) inside and outside the body's cells, which influence the storage of excess food calories as fat. Even a marginal vanadium deficiency may slow down this process and lower the fuel-burning rate. The net effect of this could be an inexplicable gain in weight. Vanadium also inhibits cholesterol formation and is important for the development of bones, cartilage and teeth.

This mineral is found chiefly in fish but it is also present in radishes, olives and vegetable oils such as corn, olive and soya. Vanadium can easily be toxic if taken in synthetic form.

## ZINC

One of the keys to good health, zinc is a vital component of the immune system which protects us from disease (it is an anti-viral agent). It is intricately involved in tissue nutrition and repair, and speeds up the healing of internal and external wounds. Zinc is essential for the proper functioning of more than 70 enzyme systems. It is a constituent of an indispensable enzyme called carbonic anhydrase, which removes carbon dioxide from tissues. It is also necessary for the assimilation of the B vitamins which are crucial to general well-being. This mineral is needed at every age and stage of life, from conception to old age. It is involved in all aspects of reproduction and can help in preventing prostate gland problems and in treating infertility. Zinc, moreover, can aid in preventing loss of taste, promote mental alertness and reduce cholesterol deposits in blood vessels. It is also needed for healthy skin and nails. A zinc deficiency can have widespread results because of the many and varied roles this mineral plays. Disorders linked to an under-supply of zinc include non-cancerous enlargement of the prostate gland, arteriosclerosis, and a lowered resistance to infection. Women bothered by menstrual irregularities might also do well to consider zinc supplementation before resorting to hormone treatments to establish regular periods.

Foods rich in zinc include brewer's yeast, cheese, eggs, lima (butter) beans, green beans, mushrooms, non-fat dry milk, nuts, pumpkin seeds, soya beans, sunflower seeds, wheat germ and whole-grain products.

# OTHER NUTRIENTS

## DIETARY FIBRE

Dietary fibre is essential for preventing constipation, symptoms of which include general malaise, fatigue and loss of energy. Studies have shown that there is a much lower incidence of health disorders such as varicose veins, haemorrhoids (piles), high cholesterol, gallstones and obesity among people whose diet is high in fibre than among those who habitually eat low-fibre foods.

Dietary fibre exists only in vegetables, breads, cereal products, fruits, grains, legumes, nuts and seeds. The major categories of dietary fibre are pectin, found in apples and other fruits, citrus peel, marmalade and jams; cellulose, the stringy fibre in vegetables which is also found in cereal foods, fruits, grains, nuts and seeds; and hemi-cellulose, consisting of a number of related substances, found in cereal and cereal products, fruits, nuts, seeds and vegetables. There are also gums, found in oats and legumes; and saponins, found in alfalfa sprouts, asparagus, chickpeas, aubergines (eggplant), kidney and mung beans, oats, peanuts, peas, soya beans, spinach and sunflower seeds.

## CARNITINE

There are two forms of carnitine: L-carnitine and D-carnitine. D-carnitine is the biologically inactive form of carnitine, while L-carnitine is the active form found in our tissues. L-carnitine is an amino acid (protein building block). Its main function is to transport fatty acids into the 'powerhouses' of tissue cells in order to generate energy.

Heart muscle contains a high level of carnitine. Medical trails have indicated that carnitine may be useful in protecting the heart muscle of people with clogged arteries. In one study, treatment with carnitine brought about improvement in tolerance of exercise. Other benefits noted in people taking carnitine supplements were an improved mental alertness and better muscle function in those suffering from intermittent claudication – a severe pain in the calf muscles during walking, which subsides with rest, and occurs because of an inadequate blood supply. Alcohol increases the need for carnitine. If you use carnitine supplements, however, use only L-carnitine.

Although L-carnitine is almost totally restricted to animal foods, humans do produce some from two essential amino acids, lysine and methionine. Three vitamins (B3, B6 and C) and iron are involved in this synthesis. Dairy products contain some carnitine, as do avocados and tempeh (a fermented soya bean product).

## LECITHIN

Lecithin breaks down cholesterol and fats in the blood, allowing them to be effectively utilized by the body's cells. Other nutrients vital for lecithin production are vitamin B6, choline, inositol and magnesium. If your diet is adequate and provides a sufficient amount of these nutrients, you can produce all the lecithin your body needs.

All unrefined foods containing oil provide lecithin. These include nuts, soya beans and wheat. Eggs also contain lecithin (the lecithin content of a fertile egg is about 1700mg).

# NUTRIENT ANTAGONISTS

Agents that counteract the health-promoting properties of the minerals, vitamins and other nutrients in the food we eat are known as antagonists.

The following are among the most notorious nutrient antagonists: aspirin, which increases the need for vitamin C; oral contraceptive pills, which act against zinc and the B vitamins; rancid oils and other rancid foods, which destroy vitamin E; some commercial laxatives, notably mineral oil, which can cause deficiency of vitamin C and the B vitamins; smoking, which destroys vitamin C and the B vitamins and reduces vital oxygen supplies to tissues; high alcohol intake, which is antagonistic to several essential minerals and vitamins; too much caffeine, which adversely affects the circulatory and respiratory systems; and lack of exercise, which impairs the delivery of vital nutrients to body tissues.

# HYGIENIC PRACTICES

## TONGUE CLEANSING

Regular practice of cleansing your tongue will help keep your breath fresh and your teeth and gums healthy. It may also prevent a sore throat developing or worsening.

### How to do it

◆ You will need a metal teaspoon reserved only for this purpose. (A toothbrush is not recommended. Special metal tongue-scrapers are available in some places.)
◆ Exhale and stick your tongue out. With the teaspoon inverted, gently scrape away the accumulated deposits, from back to front. Rinse the spoon under cool running water.
◆ Repeat the scraping once or twice, each time on an exhalation.
◆ Finish by thoroughly rinsing your mouth and flossing and brushing your teeth.
◆ Thoroughly clean the teaspoon, dry it and put it away for future use.

## NASAL WASH

The Nasal Wash is a safe, effective way to help keep your nasal passages clear and soothe the mucous membrane that lines them. It increases the tolerance of the nasal lining to various irritants, and is a splendid treatment for sinus problems and allergic rhinitis (as occurs in conditions such as hay fever). Practise doing a nasal wash up to three times a day. Do it before you begin your daily yoga session.

## How to do it

◆ Dissolve a quarter of a teaspoon of salt in one cup of warm water.

◆ Put a little of the salt-water solution into a clean, cupped hand and carefully inhale some of it into one nostril, while closing the other with a thumb or index finger.

◆ Briskly, but not forcefully, breathe out to expel the liquid. Repeat the procedure.

◆ Repeat the whole process with the other nostril.

### EYE SPLASHING

This helps reduce tension build-up in the eyes; it relaxes them and relieves eyestrain.

## How to do it

◆ Bend over a basin of clean, cool water and gently splash it into your open eyes a few times.

◆ Gently pat your closed eyes with a soft, clean towel to dry them.

◆ Rest for a few minutes, breathing regularly.

# SYMPTOMS AND TREATMENTS

Symptoms are perceptible changes in the body or its functions which may indicate disease or a phase of disease. This section deals with the symptoms of a variety of health disorders, with reference to appropriate exercises (postures) and healing nutrients. The exercises help to prevent the disorders from arising or recurring, and are also of value in assisting a return to, and maintenance of, normal function. Please remember to do warm-ups before, and cool-down exercises after the postures (see Chapter 4), and to review Chapter 2 on how to prepare for the exercises.

You will find notes on the specific beneficial nutrients after most entries – their food sources are listed earlier in this chapter. Please consult a nutritionist or other qualified health-care professional if you decide to use nutritional supplements. Remember also that all nutrients taken in through a wholesome diet work together to build health, and that no one particular nutrient is a panacea.

The treatments described in this section will help to mobilize your own natural resources – your inner healer – for maintaining good health or for regaining it. They are not intended as a substitute for competent medical care. It is imperative, in the case of all serious health problems (whether acute or longstanding) to see a doctor trained in orthodox medicine. I encourage you to combine the best that orthodox medicine has to offer with yoga therapy or other appropriate complementary therapy.

# A-Z OF AILMENTS

## ACNE

(see also *Skin Problems*)

Acne is an inflammatory disease of the oil-secreting (sebaceous) glands and hair follicles of the skin, characterized by blackheads (comedones) and red elevated areas, some of which may contain pustules. Also called acne vulgaris, or common acne. It occurs mostly in adolescence. Predisposing causes include heredity and hormonal disturbances. Food allergies, endocrine gland disorders, vitamin and mineral deficiencies and emotional disturbances are all aggravating factors.

### Exercises

Pose of Tranquillity (page 54), Pose of a Child (page 94), Half Moon (page 105), Spinal Twist (page 107), Half Shoulderstand (page 110), Full Shoulderstand (page 112), Mock Headstand (page 113), Dog Stretch (page 109), Sun Salutations (pages 49–51), Alternate Nostril Breathing (page 27), Anti-Anxiety Breath (page 28), Dynamic Cleansing Breath (page 31). Meditation (chapter 6).

### Nutrients

Vitamin A, the B vitamins (particularly B2, B3, B6, biotin, inositol, PABA), vitamins C, D and E, EFAs, chromium, copper, magnesium, selenium, silicon, sulphur, zinc.

## ADDICTION

A physical and/or psychological dependence on a substance – especially alcohol, drugs and tobacco – with use of increasing amounts. Apart from providing pleasure, many substances create dependence by altering body chemistry. Cravings increase with habitual use of the substance and withdrawal symptoms occur when attempts are made to stop.

Yoga provides safer, alternative ways of dealing with stressors. It promotes a sense of self-control and assists in resisting the appeal of addictive substances.

### Exercises

Balance Posture (page 76), Chest Expander (page 78), The Fish (page 84), Pose of Tranquillity (page 54), Sun Salutations (pages 49–51), Alternate Nostril Breathing (page 27), Anti-Anxiety Breath (page 28), Dynamic Cleansing Breath (page 31), Cooling Breath (page 32). Meditation.

### Nutrients

Vitamin A, the B vitamins (particularly B1, B3, B5, B6, B15), vitamins C and E, EFAs (omega-6 fatty acids), calcium, magnesium, selenium, zinc, carnitine.

## AIDS (ACQUIRED IMMUNE DEFICIENCY SYNDROME)

(see also *Immune System Disorders*)

Generally attributed to infection by HIV (human immuno-deficiency virus), AIDS is usually a fatal disease.

Most cases of AIDS have developed after sexual contact with an HIV-infected person. Those most a risk are homosexuals and bisexuals, particularly those with multiple partners; heterosexual partners of persons with AIDS; intravenous drug users; haemophiliacs and others receiving multiple transfusions of blood or blood products; and male and female prostitutes. There are no reports of the AIDS virus having been spread via food, coughing or talking. Some evidence does exist, however, of its spreading via tears and saliva, and an infected woman could transmit the virus to her baby during pregnancy, at birth or through breastfeeding. There is, at present, no known cure for AIDS.

Yoga can help equip you to face more courageously the many emotional and physical challenges and trials that the disease may bring. Visualization, for instance, similar to that described in Chapter 6, can be employed with benefit. You can visualize the cells of your immune system being strengthened, all the better to attack the diseased cells in your body. This will reinforce the feeling that you are doing something to help yourself, and that you are not entirely at the mercy of forces outside your control.

If you are receiving chemotherapy, practising deep relaxation (Pose of Tranquillity) and repeating affirmations during meditation can be useful in helping to alleviate nausea and other unpleasant symptoms. You can visualize your own healthy cells assisting the chemicals to do their work more effectively.

By enabling the cells of the immune system to fight the disease more vigorously, yoga may possibly help delay the onset of full-blown AIDS. Once this occurs, however, and life expectancy is reduced, it can improve the quality of life and help to diminish suffering.

## Exercises

If your energy and general condition permit, practise a few sets of Sun Salutations (pages 49–51) to begin with, followed by the Half Moon (page 105), Spinal Twist (page 107), Half Shoulderstand (page 110), or Full Shoulderstand (page 112). Finish the session(s) with the Pose of Tranquillity (page 54), or The Crocodile (page 88). All the breathing and meditative exercises are suitable for practice.

## Nutrients

Vitamin A, carotenes, vitamin B complex, anti-stress factors, vitamin C and flavonoids, vitamin E, EFAs, calcium, copper, magnesium, selenium, zinc.

## ALLERGIES

(see also *Immune System Disorders*)

An allergy is an acquired hypersensitivity to a substance (allergen) which does not normally cause a reaction. This reaction results from the release of histamine or histamine-like substances from injured cells. Allergy manifestations most commonly involve the respiratory tract or the skin.

Allergies may be inherited, or they may be triggered by pollen, dust, hair, fur, feathers, scales, wool, chemicals, drugs and insect bites; as well as by specific foods, such as eggs, chocolate, milk, wheat, tomatoes, citrus fruits, oatmeal and potatoes. Allergic symptoms are also often the body's response to stressors such as inadequate nutrition, insufficient sleep and infections.

Allergic conditions include eczema, allergic rhinitis or coryza (headcold), hayfever, bronchial asthma, migraine, urticaria (hives), food allergies, intolerances and even mental disturbances.

## Exercises

Mountain Posture (page 66), Cow Head Posture (page 67), Balance Posture (page 76), Chest Expander (page 78), The Fish (page 84), Pose of Tranquillity (page 54), The Crocodile (page 88), Spinal Twist (page 107), Half Shoulderstand (page 110), Full Shoulderstand (page 112), Dog Stretch (page 109), Sun Salutations (pages 49–51), Alternate Nostril Breathing (page 27), Anti-Anxiety Breath (page 28), Dynamic Cleansing Breath (page 31), Nasal Wash (page 173).

## Nutrients

Vitamin A, carotenes, the B vitamins (particularly B3, B5, B6, B12, B15), vitamin C and flavonoids, vitamin E, EFAs, calcium, copper, magnesium, selenium, zinc.

## ALOPECIA (BALDNESS, HAIR LOSS)

Alopecia is the medical word for absence or loss of hair, especially on the head. The condition may occur as a result of a variety of causes, including heredity, the ageing process, illnesses and infectious diseases, hormonal imbalance, nervous disorders or nervous system injury, toxic substances (such as drugs), excessive dandruff (seborrhoea), scalp injury or infection, impaired blood circulation, and inadequate nutrition and stress.

## Exercises

Abdominal Lift (page 79), Rock-and-Roll (page 48), Pose of Tranquillity (page 54), Pose of a Child (page 94), The Camel (page 99), The Bow (page 102), Half Shoulderstand (page 110), Full Shoulderstand (page 112), Mock Headstand (page 113), Dog Stretch (page 109), Alternate Nostril Breathing (page 27), Anti-Anxiety Breath (page 28), Dynamic Cleansing Breath (page 31). Meditation.

## Nutrients

Vitamin A, the B vitamins (particular B5, B9, biotin, inositol, PABA) anti-stress factors, EFAs, calcium, cobalt, copper, magnesium, selenium, zinc.

## ANAEMIA

A condition in which there is a reduction in the number of circulating red blood cells, the amount of haemoglobin (the iron-containing pigment of red blood cells) or the volume of packed red cells per 100 millilitres of blood. Anaemia is not itself a disease but rather a symptom of various disorders. It may be the result of excessive blood loss, excessive blood cell destruction or decreased blood cell formation – as occurs when the diet is iron deficient. Anaemia can also be caused by a dietary deficiency of copper, folic acid, vitamin C or vitamin B12.

### Exercises

The Fish (page 84), Pose of Tranquillity (page 54), Forward Bend (page 90), The Cobra (page 100), Half Locust (page 101), Half Shoulderstand (page 110), Full Shoulderstand (page 112), Sun Salutations (pages 49–51), Cooling Breath (page 32).

### Nutrients

The B vitamins (particularly B1, B3, B6, B9, B12, PABA) vitamins C, D and E, cobalt, copper, iron, magnesium, manganese, molybdenum, selenium, zinc.

## ANGINA PECTORIS

(see also *Heart Disease* and *Pain*)

Angina pectoris is caused by an insufficient blood supply to the heart, and leads to severe pain and constriction near the heart. The pain usually radiates to the left shoulder and down the left arm, but may sometimes radiate to the back or the jaw. Symptoms include steady, severe pain and a feeling of pressure in the region of the heart; great anxiety; shortness of breath; fast and sometimes irregular pulse rate; and elevated blood pressure. Exertion following a meal can produce angina symptoms and cold weather may also aggravate the condition.

Usually angina pain lasts for only a few minutes and generally occurs following (rather than at the same time as) physical exertion. Associated symptoms may be related to low blood sugar (hypoglycaemia), emotional upset or a heart rhythm disorder (such as fibrillation).

### Exercises

Pose of Tranquillity (page 54), Alternate Nostril Breathing (page 27), Anti-Anxiety Breath (page 28), Sniffing Breath (page 30). Meditation.

### Nutrients

Vitamins A, the B vitamins (particularly B1, B3, B5, B6, B15, choline, inositol), vitamins C, D and E, EFAs, calcium, chromium, copper, magnesium, potassium, selenium, zinc, carnitine, lecithin.

## ANOREXIA

Anorexia (lack or loss of appetite) is seen in depression, malaise, fevers and various other illnesses; in stomach and intestinal disorders; and as a result of alcohol excess and drug addiction. It is also an undesired side effect of many medicines and medical procedures.

Anorexia nervosa occurs mostly in females between the ages of 12 and 21. It develops from an intense fear of being obese, and the fear does not diminish as weight loss progresses. Usually, there is no known physical illness to account for the weight loss.

### Exercises

Pose of Tranquillity (page 54), Forward Bend (page 90), The Cobra (page 100), Spinal Twist (page 107), Half Shoulderstand (page 110), Full Shoulderstand (page 112), Alternate Nostril Breathing (page 27), Anti-Anxiety Breath (page 28), Dynamic Cleansing Breath (page 31). Meditation.

### Nutrients

Vitamin A, the B vitamins (particularly B1, B5, B6, biotin, inositol), anti-stress factors, vitamins C, D and E, EFAs, calcium, iodine, magnesium, phosphorus, potassium, vanadium, zinc.

## ANXIETY

Anxiety – a feeling of apprehension, worry, uneasiness or dread – is a normal reaction to a perceived threat to one's body, lifestyle, values or loved ones. Often it is not focused on a single identifiable cause. Some anxiety is normal – it stimulates an individual to purposeful action. Excessive anxiety, however, interferes with the efficient functioning of a person.

Anxiety neurosis may be seen in some people without organic disease. Reported symptoms include difficult breathing; heart pain and palpitations; various forms of muscle tension, including constriction of the throat and a band-like pressure about the head; feeling cold; hand tremors; sweating and agitation; nausea and diarrhoea; weakness and feeling faint; and an inability to think clearly. Rapid breathing may lead to hyperventilation which in turn leads to alkalosis, in which body fluids become excessively alkaline.

## Exercises

Pose of Tranquillity (page 54), Forward Bend (page 90), The Plough (page 96), The Cobra (page 100), Spinal Twist (page 107), Sun Salutations (pages 49–51), Alternate Nostril Breathing (page 27), Anti-Anxiety Breath (page 28), Dynamic Cleansing Breath (page 31), Cooling Breath (page 32), Humming Breath (page 33).

## Nutrients

The B vitamins (particularly B1, B3, B6, biotin, PABA), anti-stress factors, EFAs (omega-3 fatty acids), calcium, magnesium.

## ARTHRITIS

(see also *Autoimmune Disorders* and *Joint Disorders*)

Arthritis is the inflammation of a joint, and is usually accompanied by pain, swelling and frequently a change in the joint's structure.

Arthritis may result from or be associated with a number of conditions including infection, rheumatic fever, ulcerative colitis, nervous system disorders, degenerative joint disease (such as osteoarthritis), metabolic disturbances (such as gout), new growths (neoplasms), inflammation of structures near the joints (such as bursitis), and a variety of other conditions (such as psoriasis and Raynaud's disease).

Ankylosing (rheumatoid) spondylitis is a chronic progressive disease of the joints, including the sacroiliac joints and those between the ribs and spine. Ankylosis (immobility and fixation of a joint) may give rise to a stiff back (poker spine). Gout is a hereditary metabolic disease that is a form of acute arthritis. It is marked by inflammation of joints and usually begins in the knee or foot, but may also affect other joints. Osteoarthritis (OA) is a chronic disease involving the joints, especially those bearing weight.

Rheumatism is a general term for acute and chronic conditions characterized by inflammation, soreness and stiffness of the muscles, and pain in joints and associated structures. Rheumatoid arthritis (RA) is characterized by inflammatory changes in joints and related structures. It is a poorly understood condition that can result in crippling deformities, and is believed to be an immune system disorder.

## Exercises

Cow Head Posture (page 67), The Flower (page 69), Eagle Posture (page 77), Chest Expander (page 78), Pose of Tranquillity (page 54), Forward Bend (page 90), The Plough (page 96), The Camel (page 99), The Cobra (page 100), The Bow (page 102), Lying Twist (page 45), Angle Balance (page 68), Spinal Twist (page 107), Sun Salutations (pages 49–51), Alternate Nostril Breathing (page 27), Anti-Anxiety Breath (page 28), Dynamic Cleansing Breath (page 31). Meditation.

## Nutrients

Vitamin A, carotenes, the B vitamins (particular B2, B5), anti-stress factors, vitamin C, flavonoids, vitamins D and E, EFAs, boron, calcium, copper, iron, magnesium, manganese, selenium, silicon, zinc.

## Note

Avoid foods and drinks known to interfere with the absorption of minerals, such as bran, coffee and tea.

## ASTHMA

(see also *Allergies* and *Breathing Problems*)

Asthma involves sudden attacks of breathlessness accompanied by wheezing. It is caused by a spasm of the bronchial tubes or by swelling of their mucous membranes, with inflammation and the production of thick mucus. Attacks are sometimes triggered by emotional factors or mental and physical fatigue or stress. Bronchial asthma, or allergic asthma, is a common form of asthma resulting from hypersensitivity to an allergen (any substance that produces symptoms of allergy).

Regular practice of yoga breathing techniques helps to increase the stamina of your respiratory system and, as you learn to use your breathing apparatus more effectively, your tense chest muscles (and other muscles used in breathing) relax. Energy blocks are released, giving you more energy; and breathing, relaxation and meditation techniques promote calm. Some yoga postures (chiefly the inverted postures) also facilitate the drainage of accumulating mucus. In addition to helping to reduce the frequency of asthmatic attacks, regular yoga practice can be beneficial during an attack as it equips you to combat the vicious cycle of panic and respiratory distress that builds up. The increased ability to relax and control your breathing is also invaluable in preventing pains and in reducing the severity of the attack itself.

## Exercises

Mountain Posture (page 66), Cow Head Posture (page 67), Chest Expander (page 78), The Fish (page 84), Pose of Tranquillity (page 54), The Crocodile (page 88), The Camel (page 99), The Cobra (page 100), The Bow (page 102), Angle Posture (page 106), Half Shoulderstand (page 110), Full Shoulderstand (page 112), slow performance of the Sun Salutations (pages 49–51), Alternate Nostril Breathing (page 27), Anti-Anxiety Breath (page 28), Dynamic Cleansing Breath (page 31), Whispering Breath (page 34), Nasal Wash (page 173).

## Nutrients

Vitamin A, the B vitamins (particularly B6, B9, B12, B15), anti-stress factors, vitamin C, flavonoids, vitamin E, EFAs, calcium, magnesium, selenium, zinc.

## Note

Avoid monosodium glutamate (MSG) and additives with sulphur (such as metabisulphate and sulphur dioxide).

## ATHEROSCLEROSIS

Atherosclerosis refers to an abnormal thickening of arteries due to a buildup of fats in their inner walls. Although the causes of this condition are not entirely known, factors that play a part include hypertension, high cholesterol levels, cigarette smoking, diabetes and obesity.

Physical and emotional stress can accelerate atherosclerosis. Regular exercise is a splendid way to improve circulation, counteract stress and reduce the risk of atherosclerosis. Giving up smoking is also advisable. Dietary measures to combat atherosclerosis include avoiding refined foods, saturated fats and alcohol, an increased the intake of complex carbohydrates. Also suggested is the liberal use of garlic and onions, which have protective properties.

## Exercises

Chest Expander (page 78), Prayer Posture (page 71), The Fish (page 84), Half Moon (page 105), Mountain Posture (page 66), Pose of Tranquillity (page 54), Half Shoulderstand (page 110), Spinal Twist (page 107), Sun Salutations (pages 49–51), Holy Fig Tree Posture (page 73). Alternate Nostril Breathing (page 27), Anti-Anxiety Breath (page 28), Dynamic Cleansing Breath (page 31), Humming Breath (page 33), Sniffing Breath (page 30). Meditation.

## Nutrients

The B vitamins, (particularly B3, B6, B9, B15, choline and inositol), vitamin C and bioflavonoids, vitamin E, EFAs, boron, calcium, chromium, copper, magnesium, selenium, silicon, vanadium.

## AUTOIMMUNE DISORDERS

(see also *Immune System Disorders*)

There are conditions in which the body produces disordered immunological responses against itself. Normally, the body's immune mechanisms are able to distinguish clearly between what is a normal substance and what is foreign. In autoimmune diseases, however, this system becomes defective and produces antibodies against normal parts of the body to such an extent as to cause tissue injury.

Factors contributing to the onset of autoimmune disease include nutritional state, age, sex, race, heredity, radiation, alcohol intake, fatigue and stress. Autoimmune disease can occur in response to infection and as a result of treatment with certain drugs. Included in this category of disorders are rheumatoid arthritis, myasthenia gravis, scleroderma, arthritis, multiple sclerosis (MS) and lupus (systemic lupus erythematosus, or SLE).

Yoga can help you make the best of whatever muscular capacity you have. Often, this is greater than realized because when one group of muscles is impaired another group can take over. Yoga can also build the necessary courage to enable you to persevere with retraining exercises.

## Exercises

Start with gentle warm-ups and one or two sets of Sun Salutation (page 49–51), performed slowly. Add The Tree (page 72), The Plough (page 96), Angle Posture (page 106), Spinal Twist (page 107), Half Shoulderstand (page 110), or Full Shoulderstand (page 112), if your condition permits it. Daily practice of the Pose of Tranquillity (page 54), is recommended, as well as some form of meditation. Breathing exercises should include Alternate Nostril Breathing (page 27), the Anti-Anxiety Breath (page 28), Dynamic Cleansing Breath (page 31), and the Sniffing Breath (page 30) when you find deep breathing difficult. Nasal Wash (page 173).

## Nutrients

Vitamin A, carotenes, the B vitamins (particularly B1, B2, B3, B5, B6, B9, B12, B15, choline, inositol), anti-stress factors, vitamin C, flavonoids, vitamin E, EFAs, calcium, copper, magnesium, manganese, molybdenum, vanadium, zinc, carnitine.

## BACKACHE

Backache refers to the pain in any of the areas on either side of the spinal column, from the base of the neck to the pelvis. Backache is usually characterized by dull, continuous pain and tenderness in the muscles and their attachments. Pain sometimes radiates to the legs, following the distribution of the sciatic nerve.

Causes of backache include infection; tumours or other abnormality in any part of the body (the uterus or prostate gland, for example); disorders of the vertebral (spinal) column, such as abnormality of the discs between the vertebrae; bone fractures, such as those occurring as a result of degenerative bone diseases like osteoporosis; strains or sprains; inadequacy of the ligaments supporting the spine; muscle injury or spasm; inflammation of related structures; poor postural habits; and psychogenic (of mental origin) factors.

Lumbago is a general, non-specific word used to describe a dull ache in the lumbar (loin) part of the back. Scoliosis is a lateral curvature of the spine, usually consisting of two curves – the original abnormal curve and a compensatory curve in the opposite direction. Congenital scoliosis is present from birth and is usually the result of defective spinal development prior

to birth. Habit scoliosis results from habitually assuming improper body positions. Myopathic scoliosis is due to a weakening of spinal muscles. Rheumatic scoliosis is a result of rheumatism of the back muscles.

## Exercises

As a preventive measure, regularly practise the following when not in pain: Squatting Posture (page 64), Cow Head Posture (page 67), Angle Balance (page 68), Balance Posture (page 76), Chest Expander (page 78), Abdominal Lift (page 79), Knee Press (page 82), Legs Up (page 87), Pose of Tranquillity (page 54), Star Posture (page 61), Spread Leg Stretch (page 93), Pose of a Child (page 94), Triangle Posture (page 95), Pelvic Stretch (page 98), The Cobra (page 100), Half Locust (page 101), Angle Posture (page 106), Dog Stretch (page 109), Cat Stretch sequence (pages 114–115). Alternate Nostril Breathing (page 27), Anti-Anxiety Breath (page 28), Sniffing Breath (page 30). When in pain, practise Breathing Away Pain (page 35).

## Nutrients

Vitamin A, the B vitamins, anti-stress factors, vitamins C, D and E, calcium, fluorine, magnesium, phosphorus, silicon.

## BALDNESS

(see *Alopecia*)

## BLADDER PROBLEMS

(see *Cystitis*, *Incontinence of Urine* and *Urinary Problems*)

## BLOOD PRESSURE (HIGH)

Blood pressure refers to the force exerted by the blood against the inner walls of the arteries as a result of the heart's pumping action.

Hypertension is a condition in which the blood pressure is higher than that judged to be normal. Essential (primary) hypertension is that in which the precise cause is unknown. Secondary hypertension results from an underlying disorder such as adrenal gland tumour or kidney disease. Because hypertension generally produces no symptoms, millions of people are unaware that they have the condition; it is usually discovered during a routine medical examination.

Untreated hypertension can lead to serious illness such as coronary artery disease, congestive heart failure, a stroke, aortic aneurysm or other cardiovascular disease. Hypertension is one of the most difficult disorders to control since virtually any stressor will cause changes in blood pressure. The systolic arterial blood pressure, for instance, rises during activity and excitement (systolic refers to the pressure produced in the arteries by the push of the blood as the heart's left lower chamber contracts).

For many years now, yoga breathing, relaxation and meditation techniques have been used successfully to help lower high blood pressure and keep it within normal limits. The Pose of Tranquillity is outstanding among the various exercises for helping to bring about these beneficial results.

## Exercises

Pose of Tranquillity (page 54), Candle Concentration (page 121), Alternate Nostril Breathing (page 27), Anti-Anxiety Breath (page 28), Sniffing Breath (page 30), Humming Breath (page 33). All the meditative exercises.

## Nutrients

The B vitamins (particularly B2, B3, B6, B15, choline, inositol), anti-stress factors, vitamins C, D and E, EFAs, calcium, chromium, magnesium, potassium, vanadium, zinc, lecithin.

## BREATHING PROBLEMS

Breathing, or respiration, may be described as the act of inhaling and exhaling air. Exhalation is usually passive and takes less time than inhalation. When you breathe with passive exhalation, however, you do not move as much air in and out of your lungs as you can and should. The more air you move, the healthier you will be, because the functioning of all body systems depends on the delivery of oxygen in inspired air and the removal of carbon dioxide in expired air. To bring more air into your lungs, concentrate on expelling more air by attending to exhalation (see the Anti-Anxiety Breath, Chapter 3).

Various difficulties can arise during the breathing process. Here are a few:

◆ Asthmatic breathing is harsh, with a prolonged wheezing expiration (breathing out) heard all over the chest.
◆ Bronchial breathing is also harsh, with a prolonged, high-pitched exhalation.
◆ Laboured breathing (dyspnoea) or gasping for oxygen is normal when caused by strenuous exercise, but it may indicate a respiratory disorder of the amount of oxygen circulating in the blood when excessive, prolonged or occurring at rest.
◆ A breathing difficulty may be a symptom of a variety of disorders, including chronic bronchitis, emphysema, cancer or heart disease.

Yoga retrains you to breathe efficiently. It promotes mental calm, which is useful in combating such conditions as bronchial asthma. Yoga, moreover, helps to strengthen the immune system so that chronic infections are less liable to arise, but if they do, they tend to clear up quickly.

If your lungs are permanently damaged (as in chronic bronchitis), yoga practices help you to improve the mechanical efficiency of your breathing and to make the most of your reduced lung capacity. They also assist you to give up smoking.

In chronic lung diseases, such as emphysema, although yoga cannot repair damaged tissues, it can enhance the effectiveness of physiotherapy and surgical and drug treatments. Yoga breathing techniques train you to oxygenate all parts of your lungs. Some postures (such as the inverted postures) also promote the drainage of secretions and improve stamina and general health.

## Exercises

Mountain Posture (page 66), Cow Head Posture (page 67), Chest Expander (page 78), The Fish (page 84), Pose of Tranquillity (page 54), The Crocodile (page 88), The Camel (page 99), The Cobra (page 100), The Bow (page 102), Half Shoulderstand (page 110), Full Shoulderstand (page 112). Alternate Nostril Breathing (page 27), Anti-Anxiety Breath (page 28), Dynamic Cleansing Breath (page 31), Sniffing Breath (page 30), Whispering Breath (page 34). Meditation. Nasal Wash (page 173).

## Nutrients

Vitamin A, carotenes, the B vitamins (particularly B6, B9, B12, B15), anti-stress factors, vitamin C, flavonoids, vitamin E, EFAs, calcium, magnesium, phosphorus, selenium, zinc.

## BRONCHITIS

(see *Breathing Problems*)

## CANCER

(see also *AIDS*)

Cancer comprises a broad group of malignant tumours which are divided into two categories: carcinomas and sarcomas. Carcinomas originate in epithelial cells forming outer body surfaces (such as skin), and in cavities and principal tubes and passages leading to the exterior (such as the uterus). Sarcomas develop from connective tissue, such as bone and muscle.

Cancer is invasive and tends to metastasize (transfer from one part of the body to another, not directly connected). It spreads directly into surrounding tissues and may also be disseminated through the lymphatic and circulatory systems.

The exact cause of cancer in humans is unknown. Contributing factors, however, include chronic irritation, nutritional considerations, radiation, heredity and a variety of chemicals.

You can help prevent many cancers by changing your lifestyle and certain habits. For example, smoking, excessive alcohol consumption, chronic constipation and prolonged stress are all cancer inducing. With regular yoga practice you can gain control over the craving for pleasure through harmful activities that put you at risk of cancer.

If cancer does develop, yoga practices will be a useful adjunct to surgery, chemotherapy and radiotherapy. They can also be an aid to rehabilitation after surgery, but first check with your doctor.

Many cancer treatment facilities are now recommending visualization as a complement to standard medical cancer treatments. Visualization is based on principles of psychoneuroimmunology (referring to the nervous, immune and endocrine systems): what the mind visualizes can be carried out by the immune system – the body's natural weapon against cancer.

### Exercises

Practise, in slow motion, one or two sets of Sun Salutations (pages 49–51), daily or twice daily to begin with; increase the number of times according to your general condition and energy level. Follow these with the Half Moon (page 105), Spinal Twist (page 107), Half Shoulderstand (page 110), or Full Shoulderstand (page 112). Finish the session(s) with the Pose of Tranquillity (page 54), or The Crocodile (page 88). All the breathing and meditative exercises are suitable for practice. Include Candle Concentration (page 121) and Alternate Nostril Breathing (page 27).

### Nutrients

Vitamin A, carotenes, the B vitamins (particularly B3, B6, B9), anti-stress factors, vitamin C, flavonoids, vitamins D and E, EFAs, calcium, copper, magnesium, selenium, zinc, dietary fibre.

## CARPAL TUNNEL SYNDROME

(see CTS)

## CHEST PAIN

(see *Angina Pectoris*)

## CHRONIC FATIGUE SYNDROME

(see *M.E.*)

## COLDS

(see also *Allergies*, *Breathing Problems* and *Nasal Allergy*)

A general term for coryza or inflammation of the respiratory mucous membranes, known as the common cold. Chest cold refers to a cold with inflammation of the bronchial mucous membranes. It is a synonym for bronchitis. Common cold denotes an acute catarrhal inflammation of any or all parts of the respiratory tract. It is highly contagious, and caused by any one of a considerable number of viruses. Yoga practices can help reduce the frequency and severity of colds by strengthening the immune system.

## Exercises

Mountain Posture (page 66); Cow Head Posture (page 67); The Lion (page 39), particularly for a sore throat; Chest Expander (page 78); The Fish (page 84); Pose of Tranquillity (page 54); and The Crocodile (page 88); Alternate Nostril Breathing (page 27). All the breathing exercises are also appropriate. Nasal Wash (page 173), Tongue Cleansing (page 173).

## Nutrients

Vitamin A, carotenes, the B vitamins, anti-stress factors, vitamin C, flavonoids, vitamins D and E, EFAs, calcium, copper, iron, magnesium, potassium, selenium, zinc.

## CONSTIPATION

Constipation denotes difficult or infrequent defecation (evacuation of the bowels), with the passage of unusually hard or dry faecal material. It involves a sluggish action of the bowels.

It is impossible to state accurately how often the bowels should move and so to determine what is normal. The range in healthy people can vary from two to three bowels movements a day to two per week.

Factors contributing to constipation include no regular bowel movements from childhood; failure to establish definite and regular times for bowel movements; worry, anxiety or fear; a sedentary lifestyle; inadequate fluid intake; inadequate diet; internal obstruction; tumours; excessive use of laxatives; weakness of intestinal muscles; use of certain drugs; and lesions (injury or infection) of the anus.

## Note

A continuous change in the frequency of bowel movements may be a sign of serious intestinal or colonic disease. A change in bowel habits should be discussed with a doctor.

## Exercises

Efficient bowel function depends, to a great extent, on the tone of the abdominal muscles and those of the rectum and anus. Squatting Posture (page 64), Angle Balance (page 68), Abdominal Lift (page 79), Stick Posture (page 52), Knee Press (page 82), The Fish (page 84), Pose of Tranquillity (page 54), The Crocodile (page 88), Forward Bend (page 90), The Plough (page 96), Pose of a Child (page 94), The Camel (page 99), The Cobra (page 100), The Bow (page 102), Lying Twist (page 45), Half Moon (page 105), Angle Balance (page 68), Spinal Twist (page 107), Half Shoulderstand (page 110), Full Shoulderstand (page 112), Sun Salutations (pages 49–51). Anti-Anxiety Breath (page 28), Dynamic Cleansing Breath (page 31).

## Nutrients

The B vitamins (particularly B1, B5, B9, choline, inositol, PABA), vitamin C, magnesium, potassium, dietary fibre. Drink plenty of water.

## CRAMP

(see also *Menstrual Irregularities* and *Pain*)

Cramp is a spasmodic, usually painful, contraction of one or many muscles. It may be caused by heat, cold, fatigue or habitual overuse (as in so-called writer's cramp). Depending on the cause and location, trying to extend the muscle sometimes helps. The application of cold or heat is also useful. Some cramps may also be a symptom of disease, such as chronic kidney failure.

## Exercises

To improve circulation and prevent cramp, regularly practise the following for leg cramp: Ankle Rotation (page 47), Rock-and-Roll (page 48), Legs Up (page 87), Pose of Tranquillity (page 54), Forward Bend (page 90), Star Posture (page 61), Spread Leg Stretch (page 93), The Plough (page 96), Pose of a Child (page 94), Spinal Twist (page 107), Cat Stretch Sequence (pages 114–115), and, when not menstruating, the Half Shoulderstand (page 110), or Full Shoulderstand (page 112). Alternate Nostril Breathing (page 27), Anti-Anxiety Breath (page 28), Diaphragmatic Breathing (page 25). To relieve cramp use the Breathing Away Pain exercise (page 35).

## Nutrients

The B vitamins (particularly B1, B2, B3, B5, B6, biotin) anti-stress factors, vitamins C, D and E, EFAs (omega-6 fatty acids), calcium, magnesium, potassium, sodium, zinc.

## CROHN'S DISEASE

(see *Inflammatory Bowel Disease*)

## (CTS) CARPAL TUNNEL SYNDROME

CTS is caused by pressure on the median nerve at the point where it goes through the carpal (wrist bone) tunnel. It can lead to soreness, tenderness and weakness of the thumb muscles, and to numbness or tingling in the forearm, and weakness of the fingers or an inability to bend them.

The compression of the median nerve may be caused by any of a dozen factors, ranging from arthritis to being overweight. Any inflammation or abnormality that reduces space in the carpal tunnel and puts pressure on the nerve can give rise to CTS.

### Exercises

Practise daily rotation of your wrists, in both directions. Go through the shoulder warm-ups in Chapter 4. Follow this with The Flower (page 69), and finish by shaking imaginary drops of water from your hands, then fully stretching your arms sideways. Also practise the Pose of Tranquility daily (page 54), to keep the build-up of tension to a minimum. All the breathing and meditative exercises are suitable for practice.

### Nutrients

The B vitamins (particularly B2, B6, and B9), anti-stress factors, calcium, magnesium.

## CYSTITIS

(see also *Incontinence of Urine* and *Urinary Problems*)

Cystitis is an inflammation of the bladder or the ureters, which carry urine from the kidneys to the bladder. Symptoms of acute cystitis include frequent and painful urination, a feeling of urgency to urinate, low back pain, pain above the pubic area, and blood in the urine. Causes of cystitis include bacterial infection, tumour or kidney stones.

### Exercises

The Butterfly (page 44), Squatting Posture (page 64), Knee and Thigh Stretch (page 65), Pose of Tranquillity (page 54), Star Posture (page 61), Spread Leg Stretch (page 93), The Plough (page 96), Pelvic Stretch (page 98), The Camel (page 99), The Cobra (page 100), Half Locust (page 101), The Bow (page 102), Side Leg Raise (page 104), Spinal Twist (page 107), Cat Stretch Sequence (pages 114–115), Anti-Anxiety Breath (page 28), Breathing Away Pain (page 35), Dynamic Cleansing Breath (page 31), Diaphragmatic Breathing (page 25).

### Nutrients

Vitamin A, carotenes, the B vitamins (particularly B2, B5, B6, B9, B12, choline and PABA), anti-stress factors, vitamin C, flavonoids, vitamins D and E, EFAs, calcium, magnesium, selenium, zinc.

## DANDRUFF

(see *Alopecia*)

## DEPRESSION

(see also *Anxiety, Fatigue, Insomnia* and *Stress*)

Mental depression is characterized by extreme gloom. Diagnostic criteria include the presence of at least four of the following, every day for at least two weeks: poor appetite or significant weight loss or weight gain; insomnia or sleeping too much; increased or decreased activity; loss of interest or pleasure in usual activities or decreased sex drive; loss of energy and fatigue; feelings of worthlessness, self-reproach or inappropriate guilt; poor concentration; recurring thoughts of death, or suicidal thoughts.

Depression is a complex condition which may occur independent of, or together with, a physical illness – perhaps as a result of a viral or bacterial infection, a reaction to the use of any of dozens of drugs, or following the loss of someone or something that has been significant in one's life. It may also arise because of a genetic predisposition.

Hormonal shifts immediately after childbirth can make women vulnerable to post partum depression. Most at risk are those with a history of depressive illness. This condition is not the same as the 'blues' that often occur a few days after delivery. Rather, it is a frightening illness that appears between two weeks and 12 months after the baby's birth.

In the most severe form of post partum depression, symptoms include confusion, delusions and sometimes hallucinations. There may also be thoughts of harming the baby. The illness may last for months.

Post partum depression with psychotic features (such as hallucinations) should be treated immediately with appropriate medications (such as antidepressants and antipsychotic agents). Sometimes ECT (electroconvulsive therapy) is necessary, and this should be discussed at length with a doctor. For forms of this type of depression not accompanied by psychosis, antidepressants, along with other therapies (such as 'talk' therapy and cognitive therapy) have been effective.

Women who have experienced post partum depression should be cautious of taking oral contraceptives as they may contribute to further depression.

## Exercises

Graduate exercises according to your energy level. Start with the warm-ups. Add one or two sets of Sun Salutations (pages 49–51), performed in slow motion. Practise daily the Pose of Tranquillity (page 54). When appropriate, add the Angle Balance (page 68), The Tree (page 72), Balance Posture (page 76), Chest Expander (page 78), The Plough (page 96), The Cobra (page 100), Spinal Twist (page 107), Half Shoulderstand (page 110), Full Shoulderstand (page 112). Also practise daily Candle Concentration (page 121), Alternate Nostril Breathing (page 27), Anti-Anxiety Breath (page 28), Dynamic Cleansing Breath (page 31).

## Nutrients

The B vitamins (particularly B1, B2, B3, B5, B6, B9, B12, biotin, choline, inositol, PABA), anti-stress factors, vitamin C, calcium, iron, magnesium, potassium, zinc.

## DERMATITIS

(see Skin Problems)

## DIABETES MELLITUS

(see also Heart Disease and Obesity)

Diabetes is a disorder of carbohydrate metabolism, characterized by high blood sugar and glucose (sugar) in the urine. Although the basic causes of diabetes are still unknown, the direct cause is the failure of beta cells of the pancreas to secrete an adequate amount of insulin. In most instances, diabetes mellitus is the result of a genetic disorder; but it may also result from a deficiency of beta cells, caused by inflammation, malignancy or surgery.

In addition to the danger of becoming acutely ill from abnormal blood sugar levels, diabetics are also at risk of potentially serious long-term complications affecting blood vessels, nerves and major body organs.

The incidence of diabetes mellitus rises sharply after middle age. However, much of the glucose intolerance among older adults is caused by a resistance of the body's tissues to the action of insulin, and not by a failure of the pancreas to secrete enough insulin. This condition is aggravated by obesity and can often be corrected by weight reduction and exercise.

Yoga can be very useful as a complement to conventional therapy for diabetes. The self-discipline it teaches helps make diet control and weight reduction easier, and relaxation techniques reduce stress hormone levels and improve the function of the pancreas and the immune system.

## Exercises

Cow Head Posture (page 67), Stick Posture (page 52), The Fish (page 84), Pose of Tranquillity (page 54), The Crocodile (page 88), Forward Bend (page 90), The Plough (page 96), Pose of a Child (page 94), The Cobra (page 100), The Bow (page 102), Spinal Twist (page 107), Half Shoulderstand (page 110), Full Shoulderstand (page 112), Sun Salutations (pages 49–51), Alternate Nostril Breathing (page 27), Anti-Anxiety Breath (page 28), Dynamic Cleansing Breath (page 31), Humming Breath (page 33).

## Nutrients

Vitamin A, carotenes, the B vitamins (particularly B1, B2, B3, B5, B6, B12, inositol), anti-stress factors, vitamin C, flavonoids, vitamin E, EFAs (omega-6 fatty acids) chromium, copper, iodine, manganese, phosphorus, potassium, selenium, zinc, carnitine, dietary fibre.

## Note

Taking any supplement that can affect blood sugar regulation is potentially dangerous, especially in diabetics needing insulin. Such supplements should be taken only under the direction of someone knowledgeable in nutritional medicine.

## DIARRHOEA

(see also *Inflammatory Bowel Disease* and (IBS) *Irritable Bowel Syndrome*)

Diarrhoea is characterized by the frequent passage of unformed, watery bowel movements. It is a common symptom of gastrointestinal (stomach and intestines) disturbances.

Causes include faulty diet, inflammation or irritation of the lining of the intestines, gastrointestinal infections, certain drugs and emotional factors. Regular bouts of diarrhoea are also often related to anxiety and other forms of stress.

### Exercises

Pose of Tranquillity (page 54), The Crocodile (page 88). Alternate Nostril Breathing (page 27), Anti-Anxiety Breath (page 28), Breathing Away Pain (page 35), Dynamic Cleansing Breath (page 31), Sniffing Breath (page 30).

### Nutrients

The B vitamins (particularly B1, B3, B6, B9), anti-stress factors, magnesium, potassium, lecithin.

## DIZZINESS

A sensation of loss of balance, with accompanying symptoms that include feeling faint, nausea, giddiness, blurred vision and weakness of the legs. Causes of dizziness include a sudden draining of blood from the head when arising from a lying or sitting position (orthostatic hypotension); a small stroke; central nervous system disease; heart disorders; abnormality of the inner ear, where the sense of balance is controlled; certain drugs; sunstroke and food poisoning.

### Exercises

To develop good concentration and balance, regularly practise the Angle Balance (page 68), The Tree (page 72), Balance Posture (page 76), Eagle Posture (page 77) and Candle Concentration (page 121). Practise also the Pose of Tranquillity (page 54), Anti-Anxiety Breath (page 28) and Diaphragmatic Breathing (page 25).

### Nutrients

The B vitamins (particularly B3, B5, B6 B9, B12, choline), vitamin C, flavonoids, iron, potassium.

## DYSMENORRHOEA

(see *Menstrual Irregularities*)

## ECZEMA

(see *Skin Problems*)

## EMPHYSEMA

(see also *Breathing Problems*)

Emphysema is a chronic lung disease characterized by over-inflation of the air sacs (alveoli) and by destruction of their walls. This gradual deterioration of the alveoli reduces the elasticity of the lungs and the amount of the oxygen that can be absorbed with each breath. The lungs are in a constant state of inflation because of difficulty exhaling.

Common causes of emphysema are cigarette smoking and chronic exposure to air pollutants, particularly dust and fumes. Symptoms of emphysema include a breathlessness from levels of physical exertion that would have no effect on healthy people. Any effort involving the lungs – even laughing and shouting – can precipitate a coughing spell which may produce thick phlegm.

## Exercises

Mountain Posture (page 66), Cow Head Posture (page 67), Chest Expander (page 78), The Fish (page 84), Pose of Tranquillity (page 54), The Crocodile (page 88), The Camel (page 99), The Cobra (page 100), The Bow (page 102), Half Shoulderstand (page 110), Full Shoulderstand (page 112). Alternate Nostril Breathing (page 27). Anti-Anxiety Breath (page 28). Nasal Wash (page 173).

## Nutrients

Vitamin A, carotenes, the B vitamins (particularly B6 B9, B12, B15), anti-stress factors, vitamin C, flavonoids, vitamin E, EFAs, calcium, magnesium, selenium, zinc.

## ENDOMETRIOSIS

(see also *Menstrual Irregularities*)

Uterine lining (endometrium) abnormally present in areas other than in the uterus – such as in the pelvis or abdominal wall – is known as endometriosis. Although the condition is not unusual in young women, 75 per cent of women with endometriosis are between the ages of 25 and 45.

Symptoms include painful menstrual periods (dysmenorrhoea), pain during sexual intercourse, stomach and intestinal symptoms, urinary symptoms and infertility. Breast pain is another, not uncommon, symptom of endometriosis and has been linked to an imbalance of essential fatty acids (EFAs).

## Exercises

The Butterfly (page 44), Squatting Posture (page 64), Knee and Thigh Stretch (page 65), Mountain Posture (page 66), Chest Expander (page 78), Stick Posture (page 52), Knee Press (page 82), Legs Up (page 87), Pose of Tranquillity (page 54), The Crocodile (page 88), Star Posture (page 61), Spread Leg Stretch (page 93), Pose of a Child (page 94), Pelvic Stretch (page 98), Lying Twist (page 45), Side Leg Raise (page 104), Half Moon (page 105), Spinal Twist (page 107). When not menstruating, the Half Shoulderstand (page 110), and/or Full Shoulderstand (page 112), Cat Stretch Sequence (pages 114–115). Alternate Nostril Breathing (page 27), Breathing Away Pain (page 35), Diaphragmatic Breathing (page 25), Humming Breath (page 33). Meditation.

## Nutrients

The B vitamins (particularly B3, B6) vitamins C and, E, EFAs, calcium, chromium, iodine, iron, magnesium, manganese, zinc.

## EPILEPSY

Epilepsy is a nervous system disorder characterized by recurrent episodes of convulsive seizures and loss of consciousness. There are about 20 different types of epilepsy, but the seizures commonly follow a pattern of loss of consciousness followed by jerking movements of the arms and legs. They are believed to be triggered by abnormal electrical discharge from a small area of diseased or injured brain tissue.

Although the diagnosis of epilepsy is usually made in childhood, an increasing proportion of cases are now being diagnosed after the age of 50. Epilepsy that develops in older adults may be caused by tumour, stroke, head injury or brain infection. The orthodox treatment for epilepsy involves anticonvulsant medication to control the seizures.

Since the frequency of seizures is increased by stress and overbreathing (hyperventilation), yoga can play a vital therapeutic role. In particular, regular practice of controlled breathing techniques will train you not to hyperventilate, not to panic, and to maintain some balance during stressful situations. As you become adept at these breathing exercises you may, with your doctor's permission, be able to take a reduced dose of anti-seizure medications, which have the potential to produce undesirable side effects.

## Exercises

Neck warm-ups (pages 40–41). Pose of Tranquillity (page 54), The Crocodile (page 88). Alternate Nostril Breathing (page 27), Anti-Anxiety Breath (page 28), Whispering Breath (page 34). Meditation.

## Nutrients

The B vitamins (particularly B2, B3, B5, B6, biotin), calcium, magnesium.

## EYESTRAIN

A tiredness of the eyes through overuse. Stress, pollution and spending a great deal of time in front of computer monitors can all lead to eyestrain. Eyestrain, in turn, can result in other eye problems such as allergic eye inflammations. Headaches are another possible consequence.

Conscious care of your eyes can help reduce eyestrain to a minimum and so limit its potential for damage. If problems already exist, yoga therapeutic practices can bring improvement and help slow down the rate of deterioration of eyesight.

The key to improvement is relaxation. Eye muscles — like muscles elsewhere in the body — respond to stress by overcontracting. Overcontraction of eye muscles can impair focusing and distort the shape of the eyeball; it may also worsen other existing eye problems. General relaxation of the body, as well as eye exercises — such as slowly circling your eyes a few times clockwise, then anti-clockwise, and blinking several times afterwards — help to reduce tension and strain, and build up the stamina of eye muscles (refer to the 'at your desk' routine in chapter 2, pages 18–19).

### Exercises

Neck warm-ups (pages 40–41). Pose of Tranquillity (page 54), The Crocodile (page 88), Pose of a Child (page 94), Candle Concentration (page 121). Alternate Nostril Breathing (page 27), Eye Splashing (page 174), Nasal Wash (page 173).

### Nutrients

Vitamin A, the B vitamins (particularly B2, inositol), vitamins C, D and E, zinc.

## FATIGUE

(see also *Depression*, *Insomnia* and *M.E.*)

Fatigue denotes a feeling of tiredness or weariness, loss of strength or exhaustion. It may occur as a result of a variety of causes including excessive activity; malnutrition (deficiency of carbohydrates, proteins, minerals or vitamins); circulatory disturbances, such as heart disease or anaemia, which interfere with the supply of oxygen and energy materials to tissues;

respiratory disturbances; infectious disease; endocrine gland disturbances, such as occur in diabetes and menopause; psychogenic factors such as emotional conflicts and anxiety; physical impairment and environmental noise.

Chronic fatigue is long-continued fatigue which is not relieved by rest. It is usually indicative of diseases such as tuberculosis or diabetes, or other conditions of altered body metabolism.

Neurasthenia is a term previously used to describe unexplained chronic fatigue and lassitude, with additional symptoms such as nervousness, irritability, anxiety, depression, headache, insomnia and sexual disorders. It is thought to result from an emotional rather than a physical disorder.

### Exercises

Plan your exercise programme to help build up energy gradually. Start with warm-ups and short walks. As energy increases, add one or two sets of Sun Salutations (pages 49–51), performed slowly. Daily practice should also include the Pose of Tranquillity (page 54), or The Crocodile (page 88), and any of the following breathing exercises: Anti-Anxiety Breath (page 28), Dynamic Cleansing Breath (page 31), Humming Breath (page 33), Sniffing Breath (page 30). Eye Splashing (page 174). Also suggested is the daily practice of some of the following: Mountain Posture (page 66), Prayer Posture (page 71), The Tree (page 72), Chest Expander (page 78), Stick Posture (page 52), Legs Up (page 87), Pose of a Child (page 94), Half Shoulderstand (page 110), Full Shoulderstand (page 112), Candle Concentration (page 121), Alternate Nostril Breathing (page 27).

### Nutrients

Vitamin A, carotenes, the B vitamins (particularly B1, B5, B6, B9, B12, B15, biotin, PABA), anti-stress factors, vitamins C, E, EFAs, calcium, copper, iodine, iron, magnesium, manganese, potassium, phosphorus, selenium, silicon, zinc.

## FLATULENCE

Flatulence is excessive gas in the stomach and intestines, which may result in belching, bloating and abdominal pain. Gas is generally regarded as a symptom of a minor digestive disorder. In older adults, intestinal gas is likely to be because of a deficiency of enzymes needed to help digest carbohydrates in milk, fruit or vegetables. Dental defects, such as missing teeth or poorly fitting dentures, may result in improper chewing of food and swallowing of air. Gas may also be a symptom of lactose intolerance, a digestive disorder in which the enzyme that breaks down milk sugar is lacking.

## Exercises

Squatting Posture (page 64), Rock-and-Roll (page 48), Knee Press (page 82), Pose of Tranquillity (page 54), The Crocodile (page 88), Pose of a Child (page 94), The Cobra (page 100), Half Locust (page 101), Anti-Anxiety Breath (page 28), Breathing Away Pain (page 35), Dynamic Cleansing Breath (page 31).

## Nutrients
The B vitamins (particularly B1, B3, B5), vitamin K, potassium.

## GALL BLADDER DISEASE

The gall bladder is a small pouch located under the liver, and its ducts can be the site of cancerous or non-cancerous tumours, gallstones and inflammations caused by infection or chemical irritation.

## Exercises

Mountain Posture (page 66), Angle Balance (page 68), Knee Press (page 82), Pose of Tranquillity (page 54), The Crocodile (page 88), Pose of a Child (page 94), The Cobra (page 100), Half Locust (page 101), Half Moon (page 105), Spinal Twist (page 107), Half Shoulderstand (page 110), Full Shoulderstand (page 112), Alternate Nostril Breathing (page 27), Anti-Anxiety Breath (page 28), Breathing Away Pain (page 35), Dynamic Cleansing Breath (page 31), Diaphragmatic Breathing (page 25).

## Nutrients

Vitamin A, the B vitamins (particularly B3, B6, B9), anti-stress factors, vitamins C, D and E, EFAs, vitamin K, calcium, magnesium, zinc, dietary fibre, lecithin.

## GAS

(see *Flatulence*)

## HAEMORRHOIDS (PILES)

(see also *Varicose Veins*)

Haemorrhoids are inflamed and locally dilated varicose veins of the rectum or anus, which can be external or internal. They may be caused by chronic constipation, and can be painful during defecation where bleeding can occur. Yoga can help prevent piles by improving circulation to the anus and reducing constipation.

## Exercises

The Butterfly (page 44), Squatting Posture (page 64), Angle Balance (page 68), Abdominal Lift (page 79), Legs Up (page 87), Pose of Tranquillity (page 54), The Crocodile (page 88), The Plough (page 96), Pose of a Child (page 94), The Cobra (page 100), Lying Twist (page 45), Half Shoulderstand (page 110), Full Shoulderstand (page 112), Alternate Nostril Breathing (page 27), Anti-Anxiety Breath (page 28), Breathing Away Pain (page 35), Diaphragmatic Breathing (page 25).

## Note
Consult your doctor before exercising. Do not practise these or other exercises (except for the gentler breathing and relaxation exercises) if you have recently-formed blood clots.

## Nutrients

Vitamin A, the B vitamins (particularly B6), vitamin C, flavonoids, vitamin E, EFAs, calcium, copper, manganese, potassium, zinc, dietary fibre, lecithin. Drink plenty of water.

## HAIR LOSS

(see *Alopecia*)

## HEADACHE

(see also *Eyestrain*, *Pain* and *Stress*)

Headaches are usually a symptom of another disorder and can be caused by almost any disturbance.

Transient acute headaches may have a variety of causes, including disease of the nasal sinuses, teeth, eyes, ears, nose or throat; acute infections; or trauma to the head. Chronic headaches may occur as a result of a variety of conditions, such as stress, fevers, metabolic disorders or exposure to toxic chemicals.

Cluster headache is a headache similar to migraine, recurring as often as two or three times a day over a period of weeks. It tends to strike men between the ages of 40 to 60, and is thought to occur because of a blood vessel disorder. Cluster headaches usually come on abruptly and are characterized by intense throbbing on one side of the head, and pain behind the nostril and one eye. The eyes and nose also water and the skin becomes flushed.

Migraine is a sudden attack of headache, often on one side, usually accompanied by disordered vision, upset stomach and intestines, and sometimes sweating. Attacks may occur from several times a week to several times a year. The cause of migraine is unknown but is thought by some to be a blood vessel disorder. There is also a family history of the condition in more than half the sufferers.

Sinus headache involves a frontal sinus (in the forehead, over the eyes), and is best relieved by keeping the head upright. A headache caused by a problem in the maxillary sinus (in the cheekbones, below the eyes) is usually improved by lying down.

Tension headache (muscle-contraction headache) is associated with chronic contraction of the neck and scalp muscles and with emotional or physical strain.

Vascular headaches or 'sick' headaches send a throbbing pain into one or both sides of the head during an attack. They are caused by an inflammation of blood vessel walls. Migraine is the most common form of this type of headache.

Other causes of headache include poor postural habits, eyestrain, TMJ syndrome, low blood sugar (hypoglycaemia), fever, lack of oxygen, caffeine withdrawal and hangover. A severe headache in an older adult, particularly if it begins suddenly, may also be a sign of a serious condition, such as high blood pressure, stroke, glaucoma or brain tumour.

Yoga provides an effective alternative to painkillers through exercises that reduce the build up of tension and promote calm. It helps prevent the vicious circle of fear, tension and pain.

### Exercises

Neck exercises performed very slowly and carefully (Chapter 4). The Lion (page 39), Legs Up (page 87), Pose of Tranquillity (page 54), The Crocodile (page 88), Candle Concentration (page 121), Alternate Nostril Breathing (page 27), Anti-Anxiety Breath (page 28). Modify the Breathing Away Pain exercise as follows: focus attention on your hands and, with each exhalation, visualize them becoming warm (this somehow improves blood flow in the head). Meditation.

### Nutrients

Vitamin A, the B vitamins (particularly B1, B3, B5, B6, B12, choline, PABA), vitamins C and E, EFAs, calcium, iron, magnesium, potassium.


## HEARTBURN

(see *Stomach Disorders*)


## HEART DISEASE

(see also *Angina Pectoris*, *Diabetes Mellitus*, *Blood Pressure* and *Obesity*)

Heart disease is a general term used to describe any pathological condition of the heart. The most common cause of death among adults in industrialized societies is coronary heart disease resulting from atherosclerosis – a gradual build-up of fatty deposits (mainly cholesterol) on the inner lining of artery walls. It progressively narrows the arteries and decreases the blood flow through them. As blood flow is diminished, the heart muscle supplied by these arteries receives less oxygen and nutrients. Consequently, the heart muscle's ability to pump blood is increasingly threatened.

The process of atherosclerosis may begin as early as 20 years of age. Decreasing risk factors may help slow down the process. These risk factors include cigarette smoking, being overweight, lack of regular exercise, a high-fat diet and stress.

Yogic relaxation and other practices help you to develop the self-discipline you need to reduce risk factors.

## Exercises

Mountain Posture (page 66), Stick Posture (page 52), Pose of Tranquillity (page 54), Candle Concentration (page 121), Alternate Nostril Breathing (page 27), Anti-Anxiety Breath (page 28), Sniffing Breath (if the chest feels tight) (page 30), Humming Breath (page 33). Meditation.

## Nutrients

Vitamin A, the B vitamins (particularly B1, B3, B5, B6, B9, B15, choline, inositol), anti-stress factors, calcium, chromium, copper, iodine, magnesium, molybdenum, potassium, selenium, vanadium, zinc, carnitine, lecithin.

## HERNIA (RUPTURE)

A hernia is the protrusion or projection of an organ, or part of an organ, through the wall of the cavity that normally encloses it. Causes of hernia include structural weakness from debilitating illness; pressure from a tumour; injury; pregnancy; being overweight; and increased pressure within the abdomen from lifting heavy loads, or even from coughing.

Abdominal hernia is a hernia through the abdominal wall. Hiatus (diaphragmatic) hernia refers to protrusion of the stomach through the diaphragm — the muscular wall that separates the abdomen from the chest. Inguinal hernia is the protrusion of the intestine into the groin, which occurs most commonly among men. Umbilical hernia, in contrast, is more common in women than in men and describes a hernia occurring at the navel.

## Exercises

Mountain Posture (page 66) Angle Balance (page 68), Prayer Posture (page 71), Pose of Tranquillity (page 54), Triangle Posture (page 95), Angle Posture (page 106), Alternate Nostril Breathing (page 27), Diaphragmatic Breathing (page 25).

## Nutrients

Vitamin E, EFAs, magnesium, potassium. Adequate protein intake.

## HIGH BLOOD PRESSURE

(see *Blood Pressure*)

## HOT FLUSHES

(see *Menopausal Symptoms*)

## HYPERTENSION

(see *Blood Pressure*)

## HYPERVENTILATION

(see also *Anxiety* and *Panic Attacks*)

Hyperventilation is abnormally deep and rapid breathing, which results in a depletion of carbon dioxide in the blood. Symptoms include a fall in blood pressure, occasional fainting, increased anxiety, tingling of the arms and legs, headache and blurred vision.

Causes of hyperventilation cover nervous system disorders, oxygen depletion, low blood sugar or exposure to toxic chemicals. The condition may also be caused by an emotional disorder such as anxiety.

For immediate treatment, encourage the person who is hyperventilating to slow down his or her breathing, especially exhalation, or to close one nostril with a thumb or fingers and breathe slowly through the other.

## Exercises

Pose of Tranquillity (page 54), Alternate Nostril Breathing (page 27), Anti-Anxiety Breath (page 28), Whispering Breath (page 34).

## Nutrients

The B vitamins (particularly B1, B3, B6, biotin), anti-stress factors, EFAs (omega-3 fatty acids), calcium, magnesium, potassium.

## (IBS) IRRITABLE BOWEL SYNDROME

(see also *Anxiety*, *Inflammatory Bowel Disease* and *Stress*)

While the symptoms of IBS often resemble those of inflammatory bowel disease, the bowel is not inflamed. IBS is the most common disorder of the gastrointestinal tract in industrialized societies. It usually occurs in the middle years of life, developing more often in women than in men. Its key features are abdominal discomfort or pain, accompanied by diarrhoea and/or constipation. There is no known physical cause.

Movement through the bowel is controlled by the autonomic nervous system, under the influence of the hypothalamus (neural control system) in the brain. Bowel action can, therefore, be affected by your mental state — in fact, many bowel disorders are a result of stress.

Exercise is a necessary part of the treatment for IBS. By directly affecting intestinal motility, exercise can help to reduce constipation. Since exercise also reduces anxiety, it can be therapeutic in cases where IBS is stress related. Yoga breathing, relaxation and meditation practices are superb for helping you control anxiety and deal effectively with stress.

### Note

Food sensitivities may contribute to symptoms. Please consult a qualified health professional to help identify any food allergies you may have.

### Exercises

Mountain Posture (page 66), Angle Balance (page 68), Stick Posture (page 52), Knee Press (page 82), Pose of Tranquillity (page 54), The Crocodile (page 88), Pose of a Child (page 94), The Cobra (page 100), Half Moon (page 105), Spinal Twist (page 107), Half Shoulderstand (page 110), Full Shoulderstand (page 112), Sun Salutations (pages 49–51), Candle Concentration (page 121), Alternate Nostril Breathing (page 27), Anti-Anxiety Breath (page 28), Breathing Away Pain (page 35), Diaphragmatic Breathing (page 25), Humming Breath (page 33). Meditation.

### Nutrients

Vitamin A, carotenes, the B vitamins (particularly B1, B9, PABA), anti-stress factors, vitamins C, D and E, EFAs (omega-3 fatty acids), calcium, fluoride, iron, magnesium, potassium, selenium, zinc. Adequate complex carbohydrate intake.

## IMMUNE SYSTEM DISORDERS

(see also *AIDS*, *Allergies*, *Arthritis*, *Autoimmune Disorders* and *Cancer*)

Your immune system is part of your body's natural protection against environmental threats such as pollutants and microorganisms. The system consists of five types of white blood cells, bone marrow, the thymus gland, the lymphatic glands, the spleen, tonsils, adenoids and the appendix.

One of the characteristics of a properly functioning immune system is its ability to recognize a foreign agent that has entered the body and to protect the body from being harmed. Sometimes, however, the system fails. In autoimmune diseases the body seemingly wages war against itself. Some medical researchers believe that rheumatoid arthritis is a consequence of an attack on the joints by the body's immune system.

Multiple (disseminated) sclerosis, or MS, is the most common nervous system disease affecting young adults. It is also classified as an autoimmune disease.

Systemic Lupus Erythematosus (SLE or Lupus) is yet another autoimmune disorder. It is a complex syndrome which can affect many tissues and organs including the heart and blood vessels, lungs, kidneys, brain and nervous system, joints, skin and collagen (a fibrous insoluble protein found in connective tissue).

Inappropriate or excessive activations of the immune system are generally referred to as allergies — technically as hypersensitivity reactions.

AIDS severely damages the immune system, making the body vulnerable to many other illnesses, including pneumonia and cancer. There also appears to be a higher incidence of cancer among people with a suppressed immune system than among the general population.

### Exercises

The Tree (page 72), Pose of Tranquillity (page 54), The Crocodile (page 88), The Plough (page 96), Angle Posture (page 106), Spinal Twist (page 107), Half Shoulderstand (page 110), Full Shoulderstand (page 112), Sun Salutations (pages 49–51), Alternate Nostril Breathing (page 27). Any of the breathing and meditative exercises. Nasal Wash (page 173).

## Nutrients

Vitamin A, carotenes, the B vitamins (particularly B2, B3, B5, B6, B9, B12, B15), anti-stress factors, vitamin C, flavonoids, vitamins D and E, EFAs, calcium, copper, iron, manganese, molybdenum, selenium, vanadium, zinc, carnitine.

## INCONTINENCE (OF URINE)

This is an involuntary inability to retain urine, usually because of a loss of control of the sphincter muscles which open and close the urethra. It may be caused by various conditions, including a disease or injury involving the brain or spinal cord.

Stress-related incontinence of urine is leakage of small amounts of urine during coughing, laughing or sneezing. It results from increased pressure within the abdomen, in a person with weak sphincter muscles.

Urinary incontinence tends to increase with age and is somewhat more common in women than in men. A weakening of pelvic tissues from child-bearing is one cause of this, while in older women, the condition may involve a decreased level of the hormone oestrogen. In men, an enlarged prostate gland may be a causal factor, as may be a weakness of genito-urinary structures (referring to the genitals and urinary organs) following surgery on the prostate gland.

### Exercises

The Butterfly (page 44), Squatting Posture (page 64), Knee and Thigh Stretch (page 65), Pose of Tranquillity (page 54), Star Posture (page 61), Spread Leg Stretch (page 93), Pelvic Stretch (page 98), The Camel (page 99), Lying Twist (page 45), Side Leg Raise (page 104), Spinal Twist (page 107), Half Shoulderstand (page 110), Full Shoulderstand (page 112), Alternate Nostril Breathing (page 27), Anti-Anxiety Breath (page 28). Meditation.

### Nutrients

Vitamin A, the B vitamins (particularly B6), anti-stress factors, vitamins C and E, EFAs (omega-3 fatty acids), calcium, magnesium, potassium, zinc.

## INFLAMMATORY BOWEL DISEASE

(see also *Anxiety*, (IBS) *Irritable Bowel Syndrome* and *Stress*)

There are two major forms of chronic inflammatory disease of the intestines: Crohn's disease and ulcerative colitis. Crohn's disease (regional enteritis) is often found in the lower part of the small intestine (ileum), but may occur in the colon (large intestine). It commonly progresses to involve all layers of the intestinal wall. Ulcerative colitis is a disease in which ulcers develop in the lining of the colon. Please consult your doctor immediately if you suspect you may have either disorder.

Both diseases produce abdominal pain and diarrhoea which, in ulcerative colitis, is usually bloody. (Irritable bowel syndrome, while it may cause abdominal pain and diarrhoea, is not an inflammatory disease.)

Depending on the severity of the disorder, people with inflammatory bowel disease may become seriously malnourished because of poor absorption of nutrients from the intestines into the bloodstream. It is, therefore, very important to have your nutritional status monitored by your doctor (or other therapist), to ensure that your basic needs for protein and energy are being met; also to determine whether you have developed any of the numerous nutritional deficiencies that may arise during the course of the disease.

Please consider consulting a qualified health professional to help identify any food sensitivities you may have.

### Exercises

Angle Balance (page 68), Knee Press (page 82), Pose of Tranquillity (page 54), The Crocodile (page 88), Pose of a Child (page 94), Half Shoulderstand (page 110), Full Shoulderstand (page 112), Candle Concentration (page 121), Alternate Nostril Breathing (page 27), Anti-Anxiety Breath (page 28), Breathing Away Pain (page 35), Diaphragmatic Breathing (page 25), Humming Breath (page 33). Meditation.

### Nutrients

Vitamin A, carotenes, the B vitamins (particularly B9), anti-stress factors, vitamins C, D, E, K, EFAs (omega-3 fatty acids), calcium, fluoride, iron, magnesium, potassium, selenium, zinc. Adequate complex carbohydrate intake.

## INFLUENZA

(see also *Colds*)

Flu is an acute contagious respiratory infection characterized by sudden onset, fever, chills, headache, general malaise and muscle pain. Sore throat, cough and cold symptoms are also common. The causative agent is a virus of which several species have been identified. Older people with an immune system weakened by other diseases or poor nutrition are particularly vulnerable to flu.

### Exercises

Mountain Posture (page 66), The Lion (page 39) (for a sore throat), Chest Expander (page 78), The Fish (page 84), Pose of Tranquillity (page 54), The Crocodile (page 88), Alternate Nostril Breathing (page 27). All the breathing exercises are appropriate. Nasal Wash (page 173).

### Nutrients

Vitamin A, carotenes, the B vitamins, anti-stress factors, vitamin C, flavonoids, vitamins D and E, EFAs, calcium, copper, iron, magnesium, potassium, selenium, zinc.

## INSOMNIA

(see also *Anxiety*, *Depression* and *Pain*)

The term insomnia applies to both an inability to sleep, and to sleep prematurely ended or interrupted by periods of wakefulness.

Sleep patterns change as people grow older and periods of sleep, as well as total sleeping time, tend to become shorter than in younger years. This is normal and does not in itself represent a change in one's health. Insomnia is not a disease but may be the symptom of disease. The most frequent causes are anxiety, depression and pain.

### Exercises

Mountain Posture (page 66), Pose of Tranquillity (page 54), The Crocodile (page 88), Forward Bend (page 90), The Cobra (page 100), Spinal Twist

(page 107), the Sun Salutations (pages 49–51), Anti-Anxiety Breath (page 28), Dynamic Cleansing Breath (page 31), Humming Breath (page 33). Meditation.

### Nutrients

The B vitamins (particularly B1, B3, B5, B6, biotin, choline), anti-stress factors, calcium, magnesium, potassium.

## INTERMITTENT CLAUDICATION

(see also *Angina Pectoris* and *Cramp*)

Intermittent claudication is a severe pain in the calf muscles, which occurs during walking or exertion, but subsides with rest. It causes lameness or limping and results from inadequate blood supply to the leg muscles – possibly because of arterial spasms, atherosclerosis or a similar condition.

The cause and effect of intermittent claudication are similar to those of the condition that causes angina pectoris. Insufficient blood flow to the leg muscles causes oxygen starvation of the tissues, resulting in painful leg cramps that often restrict walking. After a few minutes of rest the symptoms disappear and walking can be resumed.

### Exercises

To improve circulation and prevent leg cramps, regularly practise: Ankle Rotation (page 47), Rock-and-Roll (page 48), Legs Up (page 87), Pose of Tranquillity (page 54), Half Shoulderstand (page 110), Full Shoulderstand (page 112), Dog Stretch (page 109), Sun Salutations (pages 49–51). Alternate Nostril Breathing (page 27), Anti-Anxiety Breath (page 28), Breathing Away Pain (page 35), Dynamic Cleansing Breath (page 31), Sniffing Breath (page 30). Meditation.

### Nutrients

Vitamin A, the B vitamins (particularly B1, B2, B3, B5, B6, biotin, choline, inositol), anti-stress factors, vitamins C, D and E, EFAs, calcium, magnesium, potassium, selenium, zinc, carnitine, lecithin.

## ITCHING (PRURITUS)

(See also *Anxiety* and *Stress*)

Pruritus may be a symptom of a disease process such as an allergic response, or it may arise because of emotional factors.

### Exercises

The Tree (page 72), Balance Posture (page 76), Pose of Tranquillity (page 54), The Crocodile (page 88), Half Shoulderstand (page 110), Full Shoulderstand (page 112), Candle Concentration (page 121), Alternate Nostril Breathing (page 27), Anti-Anxiety Breath (page 28), Dynamic Cleansing Breath (page 31), Cooling Breath (page 32), Humming Breath (page 33). Meditation.

### Nutrients

Vitamin A, the B vitamins (particularly B2, B5, B6), anti-stress factors, vitamins C, E, EFAs, calcium, magnesium.

## JOINT DISORDERS

(see also *Arthritis* and *Pain*)

Degenerative and other diseases affecting the tissues of the hands, feet, hips, knees, spine and other areas normally cushioned with cartilage all fall into this category.

Osteoarthritis (OA) is the most common joint disorder, and is caused by 'wear and tear' on the cartilage surfaces of joints. Factors that aggravate symptoms of OA are being overweight, poor posture, injury and repetitive work patterns (for example, construction workers tend to develop OA of the elbow and shoulder joints).

### Exercises

Squatting Posture (page 64), Cow Head Posture (page 67), Prayer Posture (page 71), Eagle Posture (page 77), Chest Expander (page 78), Stick Posture (page 52), Pose of Tranquillity (page 54), The Crocodile (page 88), The Plough (page 96), Triangle Posture (page 95), The Cobra (page 100), Lying Twist (page 45), Angle Posture (page 106), Spinal Twist (page 107), Sun Salutations (pages 49–51), Cat Stretch Sequence (pages 114–115),

Alternate Nostril Breathing (page 27), Anti-Anxiety Breath (page 28), Dynamic Cleansing Breath (page 31). Meditation.

### Nutrients

Vitamins C and D, calcium, copper, fluoride, magnesium, manganese, silicon, zinc.

## KIDNEY DISORDERS

(see also *Blood Pressure*)

Inflammation of the kidneys (nephritis), kidney stones and kidney failure are three of the many conditions that can result when the kidneys are affected. Symptoms of kidney disorder include pain, fever, swelling (oedema), disturbances in the passing of urine and blood in the urine.

Kidney stones (renal calculi) are increasingly common in industralized countries. People prone to kidney stone formation should minimize, or avoid altogether, the consumption of animal protein, and decrease their intake of fat, refined sugar, salt, alcohol and caffeine. On the other hand, they should increase their intake of dietary fibre and fluids, and drink hard water in preference to soft.

### Exercises

The Butterfly (page 44), Knee and Thigh Stretch (page 65), Rock-and-Roll (page 48), Knee Press (page 82), Pose of Tranquillity (page 54), Forward Bend (page 90), Spread Leg Stretch (page 93), The Plough (page 96), Pelvic Stretch (page 98), The Camel (page 99), The Cobra (page 100), Half Locust (page 101), The Bow (page 102), Side Leg Raise (page 104), Spinal Twist (page 107), Half Shoulderstand (page 110), Full Shoulderstand (page 112) and Sun Salutations (pages 49–51) (omit if you have high blood pressure). Alternate Nostril Breathing (page 27), Anti-Anxiety Breath (page 28), Breathing Away Pain (page 35), Diaphragmatic Breathing (page 25), Humming Breath (page 33).

### Nutrients

Vitamin A, the B vitamins (particularly B2, B5, B9, B12, choline), anti-stress factors, vitamin C, flavonoids, vitamins D and E, EFAs (omega-3 fatty acids), calcium, copper, iron, magnesium, potassium, zinc, dietary fibre, lecithin. Drink plenty of water.

## LIVER DISORDERS

The liver is responsible for most of the body's chemical activities including the metabolism of proteins, fats and carbohydrates; the regulation of blood sugar; the processing of blood components; the manufacture of bile; and the converting of poisonous substances into less harmful material which can be excreted from the body.

It is not surprising, therefore, that liver disorders can affect healthy body function in a variety of ways to produce a wide range of symptoms. These include fever, general malaise, appetite loss, weight loss, pain, anaemia, abdominal swelling and jaundice.

Cancer of the liver may be caused by some industrial chemicals, nutritional deficiencies and as a consequence of cirrhosis of the liver.

Cirrhosis of the liver is a disease marked by the formation of fibrous tissue and nodules in the liver. The causes cover excessive use of alcohol, viral infection, some medications and industrial chemicals.

Hepatitis (inflammation of the liver) is usually manifested by jaundice and, in some cases, by liver enlargement. Symptoms include headache, fever, stomach and intestinal upsets, appetite loss and itching — depending on the particular type of hepatitis. Exposure to certain poisons and viral agents are among the causes of hepatitis.

### Exercises

Mountain Posture (page 66), Angle Balance (page 68), Chest Expander (page 78), Stick Posture (page 52), Knee Press (page 82), Pose of Tranquillity (page 54), The Crocodile (page 88), Pose of a Child (page 94), Pelvic Stretch (page 98), The Camel (page 99), The Cobra (page 100), Half Locust (page 101), The Bow (page 102), Lying Twist (page 45), Spinal Twist (page 107), Half Shoulderstand (page 110), Full Shoulderstand (page 112), Sun Salutations (pages 49–51), Alternate Nostril Breathing (page 27), Anti-Anxiety Breath (page 28), Dynamic Cleansing Breath (page 31). Meditation.

### Nutrients

Vitamin A, the B vitamins (particularly B1, B2, B3, B5, B6, B9, B12, choline), anti-stress factors, vitamins C and E, calcium, iodine, magnesium, dietary fibre, lecithin.

## LUNG DISORDERS

(see *Breathing Problems*)

## LUPUS (SLE)

(see *Autoimmune Disorders* and *Immune System Disorders*)

## M.E. (MYALGIC ENCEPHALOMYELITIS)

(see also *Depression* and *Fatigue*)

*Myalgic* refers to muscle pain, *encephalo* indicates brain, *myelo* pertains to the spinal cord, and *itis* means inflammation. M.E. is thus an illness that affects the brain, muscles and nervous system, causing pain and inflammation. It is known in the United States as Chronic Fatigue Syndrome (CFS).

The most striking symptom of M.E. is severe, chronic incapacitating fatigue. For a diagnosis of M.E. to be made, however, the fatigue must have persisted for six months, accompanied by other symptoms including aching muscles and joints, headache, sore throat, painful lymph nodes, fever, muscle weakness, sleep disturbance, mental fatigue, difficulty in concentrating and mood swings.

There is still controversy over the cause(s) of ME, but research in Britain and Canada has focused on the role of enteroviruses as a primary contributing factor. M.E. can occur at any age, but is most common in young and middle-aged persons, particularly women.

### Exercises

Your exercise programme should be planned to gradually build up energy reserves. Start with gentle warm-ups and short walks. As your energy increases, add to your exercise regime the Sun Salutations (pages 49–51) performed slowly. Also suggested is the daily practice of: Prayer Posture (page 71), Pose of Tranquillity (page 54), The Crocodile (page 88), Half Moon (page 105), Spinal Twist (page 107), Half Shoulderstand (page 110) and/or Full Shoulderstand (page 112) (as energy permits), Alternate Nostril Breathing (page 27), Anti-Anxiety Breath (page 28), Breathing Away Pain (page 35), (modified to 'breathe away fatigue'), Diaphragmatic Breathing (page 25).

## Nutrients

Vitamin A, carotenes, the B vitamins, anti-stress factors, vitamin C, flavonoids, vitamin E, EFAs, calcium, copper, iodine, iron, magnesium, manganese, phosphorus, potassium, selenium, silicon, zinc.

## MEMORY, IMPAIRED

Memory has been described as the mental registration, retention and recall of past experience, knowledge, ideas, sensations and thoughts. Registration of experience is favoured by clear comprehension during intense consciousness. Retention of memory differs greatly from one individual to another.

Various memory defects occur in many disorders such as psychoses, organic brain disease and malnutrition, and as a side-effect of drugs or the result of alcohol abuse. Some types of memory loss which are temporary or reversible include those associated with epileptic seizures, head injury, malnutrition, low blood sugar or diseases such as hypothyroidism (underactive thyroid gland). Yoga practices are particularly useful for memory deficits resulting from fatigue or poor concentration.

### Exercises

Mountain Posture (page 66), Angle Balance (page 68), The Tree (page 72), Balance Posture (page 76), Eagle Posture (page 77), Chest Expander (page 78), Stick Posture (page 52), Pose of Tranquillity (page 54), The Crocodile (page 88), The Plough (page 96), The Cobra (page 100), Spinal Twist (page 107), Half Shoulderstand (page 110), Full Shoulderstand (page 112), Mock Headstand (page 113), Dog Stretch (page 109), Sun Salutations (page 49–51), Candle Concentration (page 121), Alternate Nostril Breathing (page 27), Anti-Anxiety Breath (page 28), Dynamic Cleansing Breath (page 31), Diaphragmatic Breathing (page 25), Humming Breath (page 33). Meditation.

### Nutrients

The B vitamins (particularly B1, B3, B5, B6, B12, biotin, choline), anti-stress factors, vitamins C and E, calcium, iodine, magnesium, manganese, potassium, zinc, carnitine.

## MENOPAUSAL SYMPTOMS

Menopause is that period which marks the permanent cessation of menstrual activity. It usually occurs between the ages of 35 and 58 years. Menstruation may stop suddenly, there may be a decreased flow each month until final cessation, or the interval between periods may be lengthened until menstrual activity stops altogether. Menopause can occur as a result of surgical removal of the ovaries.

Symptoms associated with menopause include hot flushes (or flashes), nervousness, excessive perspiration, chills, mood swings, low energy and fatigue, depression, crying as a result of circumstances that would not normally produce that reaction, insomnia, heart palpitations, dizziness, headache, urinary disturbances, vaginal irritation, and various stomach and intestinal upsets. Many of these symptoms are thought to arise because of a decline in oestrogen production.

Since oestrogen provides some protection against bone loss, myocardial infarction (heart attack), stroke and hardening of the arteries (arteriosclerosis), postmenopausal women are more vulnerable to these conditions (as well as osteoporosis) than women who are still menstruating regularly.

The use of oestrogen as a 'cure-all' for menopausal symptoms has been seriously questioned because of undesirable side effects and a link to cancer. Many doctors suggest a yearly pelvic examination, including a Pap test (Papanicolaou test) for detecting cervical cancer.

### Exercises

The Butterfly (page 44), Knee and Thigh Stretch (page 65), Mountain Posture (page 66), Angle Balance (page 68), The Tree (page 72), Balance Posture (page 76), Chest Expander (page 78), Abdominal Lift (page 79), Rock-and-Roll (page 48), The Fish (page 84), Pose of Tranquillity (page 54), Forward Bend (page 90), Star Posture (page 61), Spread Leg Stretch (page 93), The Plough (page 96), Pelvic Stretch (page 98), The Camel (page 99), The Cobra (page 100), The Bow (page 102), Lying Twist (page 45), Side Leg Raise (page 104), Spinal Twist (page 107), Sun Salutations (pages 49–51), Alternate Nostril Breathing (page 27), Anti-Anxiety Breath (page 28), Dynamic Cleansing Breath (page 31). Meditation.

## Nutrients

Vitamin A, the B vitamins (particularly B5, B6), anti-stress factors, vitamin C, flavonoids, vitamins D and E, EFAs (omega-6 fatty acids), calcium, iodine, iron, magnesium, selenium, zinc.

## MENSTRUAL IRREGULARITIES AND PMS

(see also (PID) *Pelvic Inflammatory Disease*)

Premenstrual Syndrome (PMS) is a group of signs and symptoms occurring several days prior to the onset of menstruation. The condition is character-ized by one or more of the following: irritability; emotional tension; anxi-ety; mood changes (especially depression); headache; breast tenderness, with or without swelling; and water retention which may cause oedema. The symptoms of PMS subside close to the onset of menstruation. It is the relief of symptoms by menstruation that distinguishes PMS from dysmen-orrhoea.

Dysmenorrhoea is painful menstruation and affects about 50 per cent of menstruating women. Amenorrhoea is the absence of menstrual flow when it is normally expected. Menorrhagia is excessive bleeding at the time of a menstrual period, either in number of days and/or amount of blood.

### Exercises

The Butterfly (page 44), Squatting Posture (page 64), Knee and Thigh Stretch (page 64), Mountain Posture (page 66), Chest Expander (page 78), Knee Press (page 82), The Fish (page 84), Legs Up (page 87), Pose of Tranquillity (page 54), The Crocodile (page 88), Star Posture (page 61), Spread Leg Stretch (page 93), Pose of a Child (page 94), Pelvic Stretch (page 98), The Camel (page 99), Lying Twist (page 45), Side Leg Raise (page 104), Half Moon (page 105), Spinal Twist (page 107). When not menstruating the Half Shoulderstand (page 110) and Full Shoulderstand (page 112). Cat Stretch Sequence (pages 114–115). Alternate Nostril Breathing (page 27), Anti-Anxiety Breath (page 28), Breathing Away Pain (to relieve cramp) (page 35), Diaphragmatic Breathing (page 25), Humming Breath (page 33). Meditation.

## Nutrients

The B vitamins (particularly B3, B6, B9, B12), vitamins C, E and K, EFAs (omega-6 fatty acids), calcium, chromium, iron, magnesium, manganese, zinc.

## MIGRAINE

(see *Headache*)

## MORNING SICKNESS

(see *Nausea*)

## MULTIPLE SCLEROSIS

(see *Immune System Disorders*)

## NAUSEA (FEELING SICK)

Nausea is an unpleasant situation which usually precedes vomiting. It is present in seasickness, often in early pregnancy, in gall bladder distur-bances, food poisoning, diseases of the central nervous system and in some emotional states such as anxiety. Nausea is also a side effect of some drugs, and a symptom of viral infection and exposure to radiation. It may even be brought on by the sight, odour or thought of obnoxious conditions.

Morning sickness refers to the nausea and vomiting which affect some women during the first few months of pregnancy, particularly in the morn-ing. Headache, dizziness and exhaustion may also be experienced. Morning sickness tends to clear up after the third month of pregnancy. In most cases, frequent small snacks of bland foods such as plain biscuits, broths and clear soups bring relief.

Motion sickness (travel sickness) occurs when motion affects the middle ear, and the vomiting centre in the brain stem is stimulated. Symptoms of motion sickness include nausea, vomiting and vertigo (dizziness) induced by irregular or rhythmic movements. Headaches may also occur.

Seasickness, airsickness and carsickness are all examples of motion sickness. Try to choose a position in the craft where up-and-down motion is minimized, avoid dietary and alcoholic excesses, reading or unusual visual stimuli. Lie flat on your back or use a semi-reclining position if you can.

## Note

Nausea with vomiting can lead to dehydration. Care should therefore be taken to replace lost fluids.

## Exercises

Pose of Tranquillity (page 54), Alternate Nostril Breathing (page 27), Anti-Anxiety Breath (page 28), Diaphragmatic Breathing (page 25), Sniffing Breath (page 30).

## Nutrients

The B vitamins (particular B1, B3, B5, B6, B9, B12, biotin), calcium, iron, magnesium, potassium.

# NERVOUS DISORDERS

(see *Anxiety*, *Depression*, *Insomnia*, *Panic Attacks* and *Stress*)

# OBESITY

Obesity means an abnormal amount of fat on the body. The word is used to refer to those who are 20 to 30 per cent over the average weight for their age, sex, height and body build.

Obesity is the result of an imbalance between food eaten and energy expended, but the underlying cause is usually complex and the condition difficult to treat. Psychological factors leading to emotional stress, a sedentary lifestyle and social problems are among the contributing causes.

Excess fat plays a role in numerous diseases, particularly among women. These include gall bladder disease, uterine cancer and osteoarthritis. It is also associated with a number of serious disorders including high blood pressure, diabetes and coronary artery disease.

A combination of regular exercise and dietary restriction is the most effective means of losing body fat and maintaining weight loss. Decrease your total calorie intake, increase your intake of dietary fibre, and reduce your fat consumption and sugar and caffeine intake. Seek help in identifying possible food sensitivities.

The discipline inherent in yoga practices will be useful in assisting you to control your eating habits. It will give you control and mastery over mental processes — such as the craving for food as a source of comfort or pleasure — and will help you to resist overindulgence.

## Exercises

Mountain Posture (page 66), Prayer Posture (page 71), Chest Expander (page 78), Stick Posture (page 52), Pose of Tranquillity (page 54), Side Leg Raise (page 104), Half Moon (page 105), Spinal Twist (page 107), Sun Salutations (pages 49–51), Alternate Nostril Breathing (page 27), Anti-Anxiety Breath (page 28), Dynamic Cleansing Breath (page 31), Diaphragmatic Breathing (page 25).

## Nutrients

Vitamin A, the B vitamins (particularly B3, B5, B6), vitamin C, EFAs (omega-6 fatty acids), iodine, iron, vanadium, carnitine, dietary fibre.

# OEDEMA (SWELLING)

A local or generalized condition in which body tissues contain an excessive amount of fluid. Oedema may result from a wide range of disorders including heart failure, kidney disease, liver disease, inflammation, malnutrition, infection and injury. It is also a side effect of some drugs.

Oedema often begins insidiously and is first noticed as an unexplained gain in body weight. Eventually it becomes apparent as puffiness in the face or swelling in the legs. Pitting oedema usually occurs in the extremities, such as the hands and feet. When the affected area is pressed firmly with a finger, it will maintain the depression produced by the finger. Elevating the swollen limb is often helpful in reducing the swelling.

Treatment of the various types of oedema requires correction of the underlying causes. In some cases, salt intake is restricted. Generally, diet should be adequate in protein and calories, and rich in vitamins and minerals (but low in salt).

### Exercises

Mountain Posture (page 66), Angle Balance (page 68), Legs Up (page 87), Pose of Tranquillity (page 54), Half Locust (page 101), Side Leg Raise (page 104), Half Shoulderstand (page 110), Full Shoulderstand (page 112), Sun Salutations (pages 49–51), Dynamic Cleansing Breath (see page 31), Diaphragmatic Breathing (see page 25).

### Nutrients

Vitamin A, the B vitamins (particularly B1, B2, B3, B5, B6, B9, B12, choline), vitamin C, flavonoids, vitamins D and E, EFAs, calcium, copper, iodine, magnesium, potassium, silicon.

## OSTEOPOROSIS

(see also *Menopausal Symptoms*)

Osteoporosis is a bone-loss disorder that affects mainly postmenopausal women and, to a lesser degree, sedentary men. The condition is marked by decreased bone density, as bone breaks down faster than it is being formed. Bone loss takes place in all parts of the skeleton, with the greatest loss tending to occur in spongy bone rather than in compact bone.

Particularly serious are bone losses in the spine and upper leg bone. The spinal bones (vertebrae) become compressed by the weight of the body when weakened by osteoporosis. Compression fractures can reduce a person's height by several centimetres.

The exact cause of loss of bone mass in older adults is unknown, but factors associated with osteoporosis in postmenopausal women include heredity, the amount of bone mass at skeletal maturity, exercise, nutrition, and hormonal influences – particularly diminished oestrogen production.

Exercise seems to help in the development of original bone mass and to retard bone loss later in life – it may actually increase bone mass in older women.

The role of nutrition in osteoporosis is related chiefly to the dietary intake of calcium. This tends to be lower in older adults and aggravated by a decreased intestinal absorption than in younger people. Vitamin D availability may also affect calcium absorption.

The use of aluminium-based antacids, alcohol, tobacco and caffeine has also been implicated in lifestyle factors contributing to loss of bone mass.

Oestrogen administration to treat osteoporosis may require special precautions in postmenopausal women who may be vulnerable to cancer. Older men with osteoporosis may be at risk of cancer if they are treated with testosterone.

### Exercises

The following postures combined with walking and other weight-bearing exercises, are useful in helping to prevent osteoporosis: Squatting Posture (page 64), The Tree (page 72), Balance Posture (page 76), Eagle Posture (page 77), Rock-and-Roll (page 48), The Plough (page 96), Triangle Posture (page 95), The Cobra (page 100), The Bow (page 102), Lying Twist (page 45), Half Moon (page 105), Angle Posture (page 106), Spinal Twist (page 107), Half Shoulderstand (page 110), Full Shoulderstand (page 112), Sun Salutations (pages 49–51), Alternate Nostril Breathing (page 27).

### Nutrients

Vitamins C, D and K, boron, calcium, copper, fluoride, magnesium, manganese, silicon, zinc.

### Note

Beware of high-protein diets which leach minerals from the body, including calcium.

## PAIN

(see also *Angina Pectoris*, *Arthritis*, *Cramp* and *Headache*)

Severe pain can produce symptoms of pallor, sweat, 'goose bumps', dilated pupils and an increase in heart rate, blood pressure, breathing and muscle tension.

Pain is considered a protective mechanism which prompts those experiencing it to seek relief and to rectify whatever is causing it. It can be acute, as in the case of an injury, or chronic, as in the case of arthritic conditions.

Medications that counteract pain are called analgesics. Used habitually they can sometimes produce unwanted side effects, and some of them are also addictive.

You may wonder why some people seem to tolerate pain better than others. One plausible explanation is the spinal 'gate control theory' of pain. Simply put, there seems to be a nervous mechanism that, in effect, opens or closes a 'gate' controlling pain stimuli reaching the brain for interpretation. This mechanism can be influenced by certain psychological factors including attitude, anxiety, tension, suggestion and personality. The doctor or other therapist who prescribes only medication for pain relief may be failing to consider such mind-generated factors.

Natural pain control methods, such as yoga practices, are largely based on closing the spinal 'gate', to influence input from stimuli reaching the brain. Compared with pain management through drugs, these natural methods mobilize the body's natural resources to promote comfort and a sense of well-being.

Yoga recognizes the very close relationship between our respiratory (breathing) system and the perception of and reaction to pain. When we are uncomfortable or in pain, our breathing speeds up and becomes shallow, difficult or irregular. When we are at ease, however, our breathing tends to be slower and more regular. Yoga breathing techniques teach you how to bring pain under your own conscious, wilful control. They show you how to slow down your breathing to lessen tension and anxiety, and in doing so ease discomfort and pain. They also provide a mental diversion from the pain itself so that it is perceived as less intense.

People who exercise regularly tend to cope better with pain than those who do not. Regular exercise produces more of the body's natural pain relievers (endorphins and enkephalins).

## Exercises

The Tree (page 72), Balance Posture (page 76), Eagle Posture (page 77), Candle Concentration (page 121), Alternate Nostril Breathing (page 27) (which train you in mental steadiness). Pose of Tranquillity (page 54), The Crocodile (page 88), Pose of a Child (page 94) (which discourage tension build-up and promote relaxation). All the breathing exercises (particularly Breathing Away Pain, page 35) are suitable. Meditation.

## Nutrients

Vitamin A, the B vitamins (particularly B1, B3, B6, B9, B12, biotin), anti-stress factors, vitamins C, D and E, EFAs, calcium, copper, magnesium, selenium.

# PANIC ATTACKS

(see also *Anxiety* and *Hyperventilation*)

A panic attack is an acute attack of anxiety, terror or fright, usually of sudden onset, and which may be uncontrollable enough to require sedation. Panic attack symptoms include racing or pounding heartbeat, chest pain, dizziness, feeling of lightheadedness, nausea, difficult breathing, tingling or numbness in the hands and dream-like sensations or perceptual distortions.

A panic attack typically lasts for several minutes and is one of the most distressing conditions a person can experience. People who experience repeated panic attacks are said to have a panic disorder. This condition is usually treated with a combination of medication and psychotherapy.

One immediate and effective way to relieve the hyperventilation that accompanies a panic attacks is to instruct the individual experiencing it to breathe through one nostril while closing the mouth and the other nostril.

## Exercises

Mountain Posture (page 66), The Tree (page 72), Balance Posture (page 76), Eagle Posture (page 77) (to help develop mental steadiness). Chest Expander (page 78), Stick Posture (page 52), Pose of Tranquillity (page 54), The Crocodile (page 88), Alternate Nostril Breathing (page 27), Anti-Anxiety Breath (also useful during an attack) (page 28), Diaphragmatic Breathing (page 25), Humming Breath (page 33), Whispering Breath (page 34). Meditation.

## Nutrients

The B vitamins (particularly B1, B2, B6, biotin), anti-stress factors, EFAs, calcium, magnesium.

## PID (PELVIC INFLAMMATORY DISEASE)

(see also *Menstrual Irregularities* and *Pain*)

PID is ascending infection from the vagina or cervix to the uterus and its attachments – particularly the fallopian tubes. Symptoms include purulent vaginal discharge, abdominal pain, fever, chills, nausea, vomiting and general weakness. Almost any bacterium (germ) can cause PID, but the most frequent agents are Neisseria gonorrhoea and Chlamydia trachomatis. PID may also result from the insertion of an intra-uterine contraceptive device, from an abortion or from sexual intercourse with a man who has a sexually transmitted disease.

### Exercises

The following exercises, practised regularly, are useful for maintaining pelvic and general health: The Butterfly (page 44), Squatting Posture (page 64), Knee and Thigh Stretch (page 65), Mountain Posture (page 66), Chest Expander (page 78), Knee Press (page 82), Pose of Tranquillity (page 54), The Crocodile (page 88), Star Posture (page 61), Spread Leg Stretch (page 93), Pose of a Child (page 94), Pelvic Stretch (page 98), The Camel (page 99), Lying Twist (page 45), Side Leg Raise (page 104), Spinal Twist (page 107), Cat Stretch Sequence (page 114–115). Alternate Nostril Breathing (page 27), Anti-Anxiety Breath (page 28), Breathing Away Pain (page 35), Diaphragmatic Breathing (page 25), Humming Breath (page 33). Meditation.

### Nutrients

Vitamin A, the B vitamins (particularly B2, B3, B5, B6, B9, B12), vitamins C and E, EFAs (omega-6 fatty acids), zinc.

## PILES

(see *Haemorrhoids*)

## PMS

(see *Menstrual Irregularities*)

## PROSTATE GLAND DISORDERS

The prostate gland encircles the neck of the bladder and urethra in the male. The gland secretes a thin, opalescent, slightly alkaline fluid that forms part of semen.

Enlargement of the prostate gland is common, especially after middle age. This causes troublesome symptoms such as the need to urinate frequently (often at night), an inability to completely empty the bladder, and difficulty or pain in urinating.

Cancer of the prostate is the second most common cancer in men, especially after 50 years of age. The cause is unknown, but sex hormones and viruses may play a part. After its symptomless early stages, cancer of the prostate produces the same symptoms as an enlarged prostate, when the growing tumour restricts the normal flow of urine. There may also be blood in the urine.

### Exercises

The following exercises, practised regularly, are useful for maintaining pelvic and general health: The Butterfly (page 44), Squatting Posture (page 64), Knee and Thigh Stretch (page 65), Mountain Posture (page 66), Chest Expander (page 78), Knee Press (page 82), Pose of Tranquillity (page 54), The Crocodile (page 88), Star Posture (page 61), Spread Leg Stretch (page 93), Pose of a Child (page 94), Pelvic Stretch (page 98), The Camel (page 99), Lying Twist (page 45), Side Leg Raise (page 104), Spinal Twist (page 107), Cat Stretch Sequence (page 114–115). Alternate Nostril Breathing (page 27), Breathing Away Pain (page 35), Dynamic Cleansing Breath (page 31), Humming Breath (page 33).

### Nutrients

Vitamin A, the B vitamins (particularly B2, B3, B5, B6, B9, B12), vitamins C and E, EFAs (omega-6 fatty acids), zinc.

## REPRODUCTIVE PROBLEMS

Reproductive problems often have a marked psychological component. For example, fear, guilt or resentment related to genital functions can generate sexual difficulties in both sexes. In women, stress, subconscious needs and suppressed emotions can all produce menstrual problems. Obtaining help in identifying underlying causes of reproductive problems is an excellent first step towards overcoming these ailments.

Yoga trains you to develop an awareness of your inner needs, and equips you to deal with them constructively. It can assist you to overcome physical obstacles that interfere with good health, and provide the body with reinforcement for healing itself. The many breathing, relaxation and meditation techniques are also excellent tools for helping you deal effectively with stress.

## Exercises

The Butterfly (page 44), Squatting Posture (page 64), Knee and Thigh Stretch (page 65), Mountain Posture (page 66), Angle Balance (page 68), Abdominal Lift (page 79), The Fish (page 84), Pose of Tranquillity (page 54), The Crocodile (page 88), Star Posture (page 61), Spread Leg Stretch (page 93), Pose of a Child (page 94), Pelvic Stretch (page 98), The Camel (page 99), The Cobra (page 100), Half Locust (page 101), The Bow (page 102), Side Leg Raise (page 104), Spinal Twist (page 107), Half Shoulderstand (page 110), Full Shoulderstand (page 112), Alternate Nostril Breathing (page 27), Anti-Anxiety Breath (page 28), Dynamic Cleansing Breath (page 31). Meditation.

## Nutrients

Vitamin A, the B vitamins (particularly B2, B3, B6), anti-stress factors, vitamins C and E, EFAs, calcium, chromium, iron, magnesium, manganese, molybdenum, selenium, zinc, carnitine.

## SEIZURES

(see *Epilepsy*)

## SEXUAL PROBLEMS

(see *Reproductive Problems*)

## SKIN PROBLEMS

(see also *Allergies* and *Itching*)

Some skin problems respond well to simple treatments and minor changes in diet. Others require medications and therapies best given or recommended by a medical doctor or dermatologist.

Acne – for information, see the specific entry.

Eczema (dermatitis) generally refers to inflammation of the skin. It largely results from an irritant such as a chemical or cosmetic, but can also be triggered by too much heat, sweating, substances producing allergy (allergens), infection and emotional stress. (Emotional stress is possibly the most potent trigger).

Psoriasis is a chronic, recurring, non-contagious condition which is thought to be inherited. The course of this disorder is affected by injury, infection, stress and drugs.

Rash is a word generally applied to any 'breaking out' of the skin, especially in connection with contagious diseases. It is one of the most common side effects of a number of medications.

Wrinkling of the skin, if permanent, may be the result of ageing. If temporary, it can be due to prolonged immersion in water or dehydration.

## Exercises

(see *Acne*)

## Nutrients

(see *Acne*)

## SLE (SYSTEMIC LUPUS ERYTHEMATOSUS)

(see *Immune System Disorder*)

## STOMACH DISORDERS

(see also *Flatulence* and *Ulcers*)

Acid stomach is the return of digestive acid into the mouth, or excessive production of stomach acid. There is often a burning sensation (heartburn) in the 'food-pipe' (oesophagus) as well as belching.

Dyspepsia (indigestion) refers to imperfect or painful digestion. Usually symptomatic of other disorders, it is characterized by vague abdominal discomfort, belching, heartburn, loss of appetite, weight loss, nausea or vomiting. Symptoms increase in times of stress. Digestive system diseases that cause indigestion include peptic ulcers, gall bladder disease and hiatus (diaphragmatic) hernia.

Gastritis is inflammation of the stomach, characterized by pain or tenderness in the area of the stomach as well as by nausea and vomiting. The causes are generally unknown, but the condition may result from infection, excessive alcohol intake and dietary indiscretions, or it can be because of an excess or deficiency of stomach acid.

### Exercises

Mountain Posture (page 66), Angle Balance (page 68), The Tree (page 72), Chest Expander (page 78), Stick Posture (page 52), Pose of Tranquillity (page 54), The Crocodile (page 88), Candle Concentration (page 121), Alternate Nostril Breathing (page 27), Anti-Anxiety Breath (page 28), Diaphragmatic Breathing (page 25), Humming Breath (page 33). Meditation.

### Nutrients

Vitamin A, the B vitamins (particularly B1, B2, B3, B5, B6, B9, choline, PABA), anti-stress factors, vitamins C, E and K, calcium, magnesium, manganese, potassium.

## STRESS

(see also *Anxiety*, *Insomnia* and *Panic Attacks*)

Stress is the non-specific response by the body to any demand made upon it. It becomes a problem when demands tax or exceed our adaptive resources. When people are under stress various changes take place in the body. These include increased muscle tension (such as a tight jaw and rigid back muscles), faster pulse rate, elevated blood pressure, faster rate of breathing, impairment of digestion, shortened blood clotting time, withdrawal of minerals from bones, mobilization of fats from storage deposits and retention of an abnormal amount of salt.

Any event, circumstance or other agent causing or leading to stress is called a stressor. Stressors include fear, guilt, regret, frustration and uncertainty. They can have a great impact on the immune system and seriously undermine health. The key to managing stress effectively is to maintain a high standard of health. Inherent in this is the daily practice of some form of relaxation.

### Exercises

Mountain Posture (page 66), The Tree (page 72), Chest Expander (page 78), Rock-and-Roll (page 48), Pose of Tranquillity (page 54), The Crocodile (page 88), The Plough (page 96), Pose of a Child (page 94), The Cobra (page 100), Half Moon (page 105), Spinal Twist (page 107), Half Shoulderstand (page 110), Full Shoulderstand (page 112), Sun Salutations (pages 49–51), Alternate Nostril Breathing (page 27), Anti-Anxiety Breath (page 28), Dynamic Cleansing Breath (page 31), Sniffing Breath (page 30), Humming Breath (page 33). Meditation.

### Nutrients

Vitamin A, the B vitamins (particularly B2, B3, B5, B6, choline), anti-stress factors, vitamin C, flavonoids, vitamins D and E, EFAs, calcium, magnesium, manganese, potassium, silicon.

## STRESS-RELATED INCONTINENCE

(see *Incontinence of urine*)

## SWELLING

(see *Oedema*)

complete yoga

## TENSION

(see *Stress*)

## THYROID GLAND PROBLEMS

The thyroid gland is a gland of internal secretion, located in the base of the neck. It secretes the hormone thyroxin.

Goitre is an enlargement of the thyroid gland. It may occur because of a lack of iodine in the diet, inflammation from infection or either an under or over-functioning of the gland.

Hypothyroidism is caused by a deficiency of thyroid secretion, and results in lowered basal metabolism. Symptoms may include dry skin and hair, obesity, slow pulse, low blood pressure and sluggishness of all functions.

Thyrotoxicosis is a toxic condition resulting from overactivity of the thyroid gland. Symptoms include rapid heart action, tremors, enlargement of the gland, abnormal protrusion of the eyeballs, nervous symptoms and weight loss.

### Exercises

Pose of Tranquillity (page 54), Pose of a Child (page 94), Spinal Twist (page 107), Half Shoulderstand (page 110), Full Shoulderstand (page 112), Mock Headstand (page 113), Sun Salutations (pages 49–51), Alternate Nostril Breathing (page 27), Anti-Anxiety Breath (page 28), Dynamic Cleansing Breath (page 31). Meditation.

### Nutrients

Vitamins A, carotenes, the B vitamins (particularly B2, B5, B6, choline), anti-stress factors, vitamins C and E, EFAs, chromium, iodine, manganese, selenium, zinc, dietary fibre.

## TMJ (TEMPOROMANDIBULAR JOINT) SYNDROME

(see also *Pain* and *Stress*)

TMJ syndrome refers to pain and inflammation in the jaw joints (temporomandibular) and adjoining muscles. The pain worsens with chewing, and clicking sounds can be heard. There may also be ringing in the ears (tinnitus).

One cause of TMJ syndrome is grinding the teeth and contracting the jaw muscles in an unconscious attempt to relieve muscle tension generated by stress. Other causes include ill-fitting dentures or an attempt to compensate for a faulty alignment ('bite') between the upper and lower jaw. The condition is more common in women than in men, and the risk of TMJ syndrome increases with osteoarthritis and stress. Preventive measures include refraining from grinding the teeth, and the regular practice of tension-relieving exercises.

### Exercises

The Lion (page 39), following neck and shoulder warm-ups (pages 40–42). Be aware of tension accumulating in your jaw: unclench your teeth. Practice the Pose of Tranquillity (page 54) daily, as well as breathing exercises: Anti-Anxiety Breath (page 28), Dynamic Cleansing Breath (page 31), Diaphragmatic Breathing (page 25), Humming Breath (page 33), Sniffing Breath (page 30). Meditation.

### Nutrients

The B vitamins (particularly B5), anti-stress factors, calcium, magnesium.

## ULCERS (DUODENAL, GASTRIC, PEPTIC)

A gastric ulcer is an ulcer of the mucous membrane lining the stomach. A duodenal ulcer is an ulcer of the first part of the small intestine (duodenum). Both are caused by the action of acidic stomach (gastric) secretions.

The term peptic ulcer refers to ulceration of either the stomach or the duodenum. Stress ulcer refers to a peptic ulcer caused by acute or chronic stress, and is seen following some surgical procedures and in conditions that include brain trauma, burns, acute infection, prolonged treatment with steroids and central nervous system diseases.

### Exercises

Mountain Posture (page 66), The Tree (page 72), Chest Expander (page 78), Stick Posture (page 52), Pose of Tranquillity (page 54), The Crocodile (page that include brain trauma, burns, acute infection, prolonged treatment with steroids and central nervous system diseases.

## Exercises

Mountain Posture (page 66), The Tree (page 72), Chest Expander (page 78), Stick Posture (page 52), Pose of Tranquillity (page 54), The Crocodile (page 88), Pose of a Child (page 94), Sun Salutations (pages 49–51), Candle Concentration (page 121), Alternate Nostril Breathing (page 27). Anti-Anxiety Breath (page 28), Humming Breath (page 33). Meditation.

## Nutrients

Vitamin A, the B vitamins (particularly B6), anti-stress factors, vitamins E and K, EFAs, iron (if anaemia occurs, or if there is a tendency thereto).

## URINARY PROBLEMS

(see *Cystitis*, *Incontinence of Urine* and *Prostate Gland Disorders*)

## VARICOSE VEINS

Enlarged, twisted, superficial veins that may occur in almost any part of the body but are mostly seen in the legs. The main cause is incompetent valves of the veins, which may have been present at birth or acquired. The development of varicose veins is promoted and aggravated by pregnancy, obesity and occupations requiring prolonged standing.

Preventive measures include avoiding anything that impedes the return of blood in the veins (such as the wearing of tight girdles), crossing the legs at the knees, prolonged sitting, prolonged standing and being overweight.

Check with your doctor for permission to do the exercises in this book.

## Exercises

See general cautions (Chapter 2). Legs Up (page 87), Pose of Tranquillity (page 54), Half Shoulderstand (page 100), Full Shoulderstand (page 112), Alternate Nostril Breathing (page 27), Diaphragmatic Breathing (page 25), Humming Breath (page 33).

## Nutrients

Vitamin A, the B vitamins (particularly B6), vitamin C, flavonoids, vitamin E, EFAs, calcium, copper, magnesium, zinc, dietary fibre, lecithin.

## WEIGHT PROBLEMS

(see *Anorexia* and *Obesity*)

## WIND (GAS)

(see *Flatulence*)

## WRINKLES

(see *Skin Problems*)

# GLOSSARY

|  |  |
|---|---|
| Adrenal glands | Two small triangular-shaped endocrine glands, one above each kidney. |
| Allergen | Any substance that causes manifestations of allergy. |
| Alveoli | Air cells of the lungs. |
| Amino acids | Protein building blocks. |
| Anaemia | Deficiency in either the quality or quantity of red blood cells. |
| Anaesthesia | Partial or complete loss of sensation, with or without loss of consciousness. |
| Analgesic | A remedy that relieves pain. |
| Angina | Usually refers to 'angina pectoris', which is severe pain and constriction about the heart. |
| Antenatal | Occurring before birth. |
| Antioxidant | An agent that prevents or inhibits oxidation. |
| Arteriosclerosis | A gradual loss of elasticity in the walls of arteries due to thickening and calcification. |
| Atherosclerosis | A form of arteriosclerosis, characterized by a build-up of fatty material within the arteries. |
| Asana | A yoga physical exercise. A posture comfortably held. |
| Autonomic nervous system | The part of the nervous system that is concerned with control of involuntary body functions. |
| Bronchi | The two main branches leading from the trachea (windpipe) to the lungs, providing the passageway for air movement (singular, bronchus). |
| Cardiovascular | Pertains to the heart and blood vessels. |
| Cartilage | Gristle. A specialized type of connective tissue forming parts of the skeleton, and covering the ends of bones. |
| Cholesterol | A sterol (fat) widely distributed in animal tissues, oils and other foods. Also found in various parts of the human body. |
| Chronic | Of long duration. Refers to a disease showing little change, or of slow progression. |
| Collagen | A fibrous insoluble protein found in connective tissue, including skin. |
| Connective tissue | Tissue that supports and connects other tissues and body parts. |
| Coronary | Refers to the heart. |
| Defecation | Evacuation of the bowels. |
| Diaphragm | Dome-shaped muscle of respiration, separating the chest and abdominal cavities, with its convexity upwards. It contracts with each inspiration (inward breath) and relaxes with each expiration (outward breath). |
| Discs | Refers to spinal discs, which cushion the bones making up the spine (vertebrae). |
| Diuretic | An agent that increases the secretion of urine. |
| Dyspnoea | Air hunger resulting in laboured or difficult breathing; sometimes accompanied by pain. |
| Endocrine glands | Glands whose secretions (hormones) flow directly into the blood and are circulated to all parts of the body. |

| | |
|---|---|
| Enzyme | A complex protein that is capable of inducing chemical changes in other substances without being changed itself. |
| Expiration | The expulsion of air from the lungs in breathing. |
| Gastrointestinal | Pertains to the stomach and intestine. |
| Haemoglobin | The iron-containing pigment of red blood cells |
| Hamstring muscles | Three muscles at the back of the thighs. They flex the legs, and extend the thighs and draw them towards the midline of the body. |
| Hormone | A chemical substance which is generated in one organ and carried by the blood to another, in which it excites activity. A secretion of endocrine glands. |
| Hypertension | High blood pressure. |
| Hyperventilation | Overbreathing, as occurs in forced respiration. Results in carbon dioxide depletion with several accompanying symptoms including a fall in blood pressure, anxiety and sometimes fainting. |
| Immune system | The body's chief specific defence against disease and other foreign agents. It includes white blood cells, bone marrow, the lymphatic system, the spleen and the thymus gland. |
| Legumes | Fruits or pods of beans, peas or lentils. |
| Lumbar | Pertaining to the loins. The part of the back between the chest and pelvis. |
| Lymph | The fluid from the blood which has passed through the walls of capillaries (tiny blood vessels) to supply nutrients to tissue cells. |
| Metabolic | Pertains to metabolism. |
| Metabolism | The sum of all physical and chemical changes that take place within an organism. |
| Mnemonic | Refers to memory. A device to aid the memory. |
| Modality | A method of application or the employment of any therapeutic agent, limited usually to physical agents. |
| Mucous membrane | Membrane lining passages and cavities communicating with the air (such as the nose). |
| Mucus | Viscid fluid secreted by mucous membrane. |
| Oestrogen | An endocrine secretion which stimulates the female generative organs to reproductive function. |
| Oxidation | The process of a substance combining with oxygen. |
| Postnatal | After birth. |
| Postpartum | Occurring after childbirth. |
| Pranayama | Refers to the integration of the nervous and respiratory systems. Breathing exercises. |
| Prone | Lying on the abdomen; face downwards. |
| Psychoprophylaxis | From Greek 'psyche', meaning mind, and 'prophylactikos' meaning guarding. Describes a method of mental and physical preparation for natural childbirth. |
| Psyche | All that constitutes the mind and its processes. |
| Respiration | Breathing, that is, inspiration and expiration. |
| Respiratory | Pertaining to respiration. |
| Skeletal | Pertaining to the skeleton or the body's bony framework. |
| Vertebrae | The thirty-three irregular bones forming the spinal column (singular, vertebra). |
| Vertebral column | Spine or spinal column. |

# INDEX

c o m p l e t e   y o g a